SPIDER-MAN
DOCTOR OCTOPUS
YEAR ONE

SPID

DOCTO

YEA

R-MAN
OCTOPUS
R ONE

WRITER: **ZEB WELLS**
ARTIST: **KAARE ANDREWS**
COLORS: **JOSE VILLARRUBIA**

LETTERERS: **VIRTUAL CALLIGRAPHY'S DAVE SHARPE**
EDITOR: **WARREN SIMONS**
EXECUTIVE EDITOR: **AXEL ALONSO**

COLLECTION EDITOR: **JENNIFER GRÜNWALD**
SENIOR EDITOR, SPECIAL PROJECTS: **JEFF YOUNGQUIST**
DIRECTOR OF SALES: **DAVID GABRIEL**
PRODUCTION: **LORETTA KROL**
BOOK DESIGNER: **CARRIE BEADLE**
CREATIVE DIRECTOR: **TOM MARVELLI**

EDITOR IN CHIEF: **JOE QUESADA**
PUBLISHER: **DAN BUCKLEY**

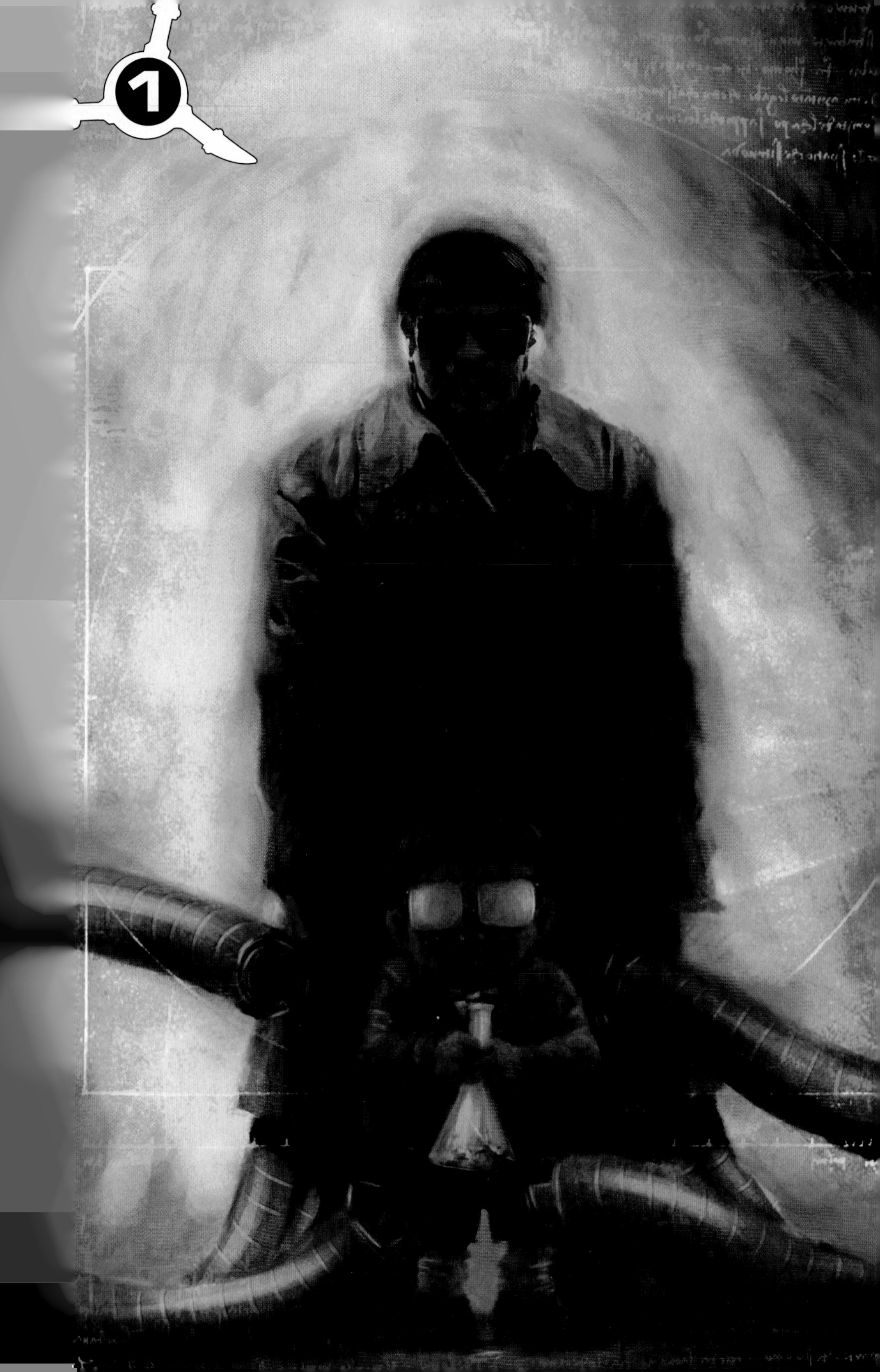
1

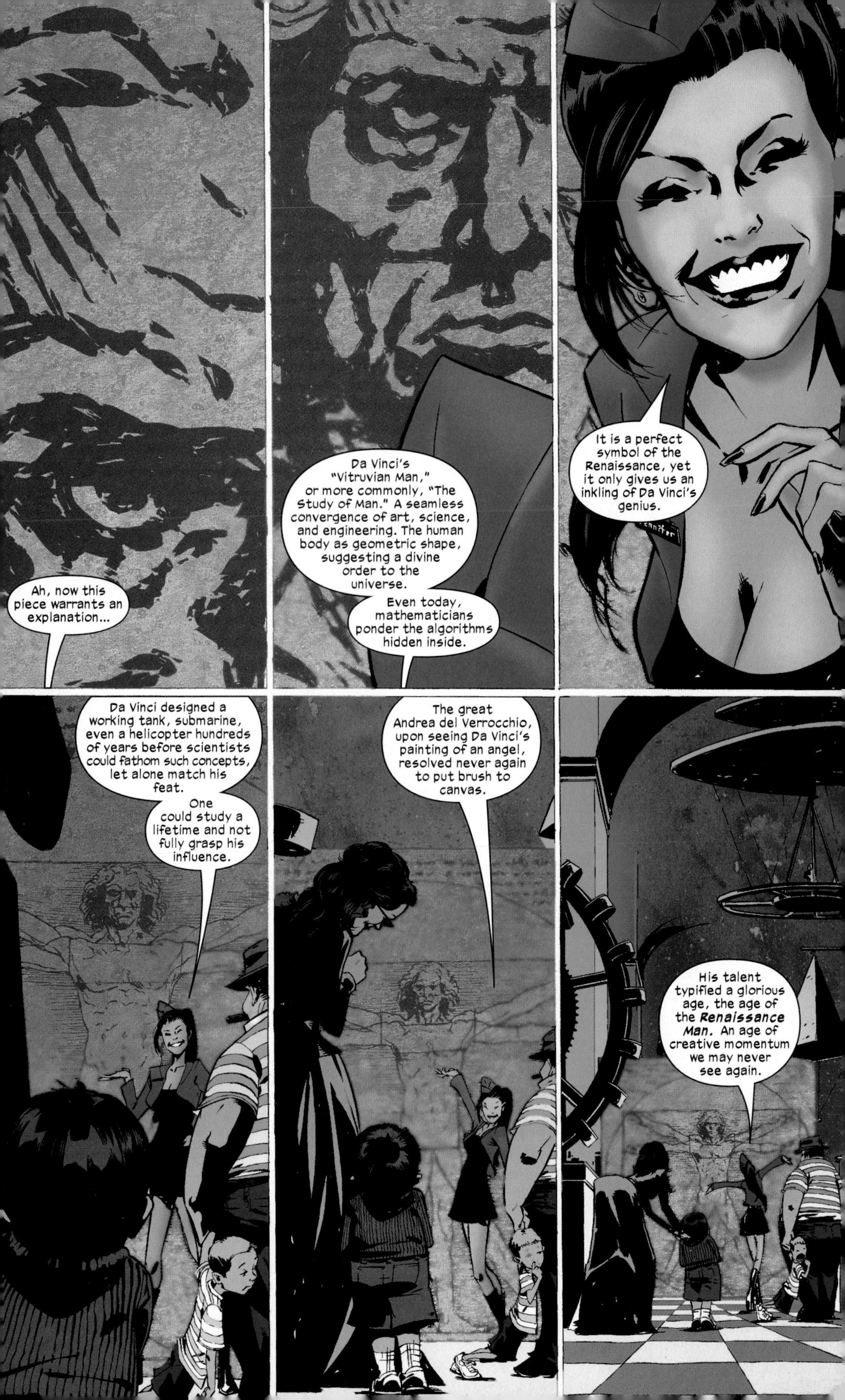
Ah, now this piece warrants an explanation...
Da Vinci's "Vitruvian Man," or more commonly, "The Study of Man." A seamless convergence of art, science, and engineering. The human body as geometric shape, suggesting a divine order to the universe.
Even today, mathematicians ponder the algorithms hidden inside.
It is a perfect symbol of the Renaissance, yet it only gives us an inkling of Da Vinci's genius.
Da Vinci designed a working tank, submarine, even a helicopter hundreds of years before scientists could fathom such concepts, let alone match his feat.
One could study a lifetime and not fully grasp his influence.
The great Andrea del Verrocchio, upon seeing Da Vinci's painting of an angel, resolved never again to put brush to canvas.
His talent typified a glorious age, the age of the *Renaissance Man.* An age of creative momentum we may never see again.

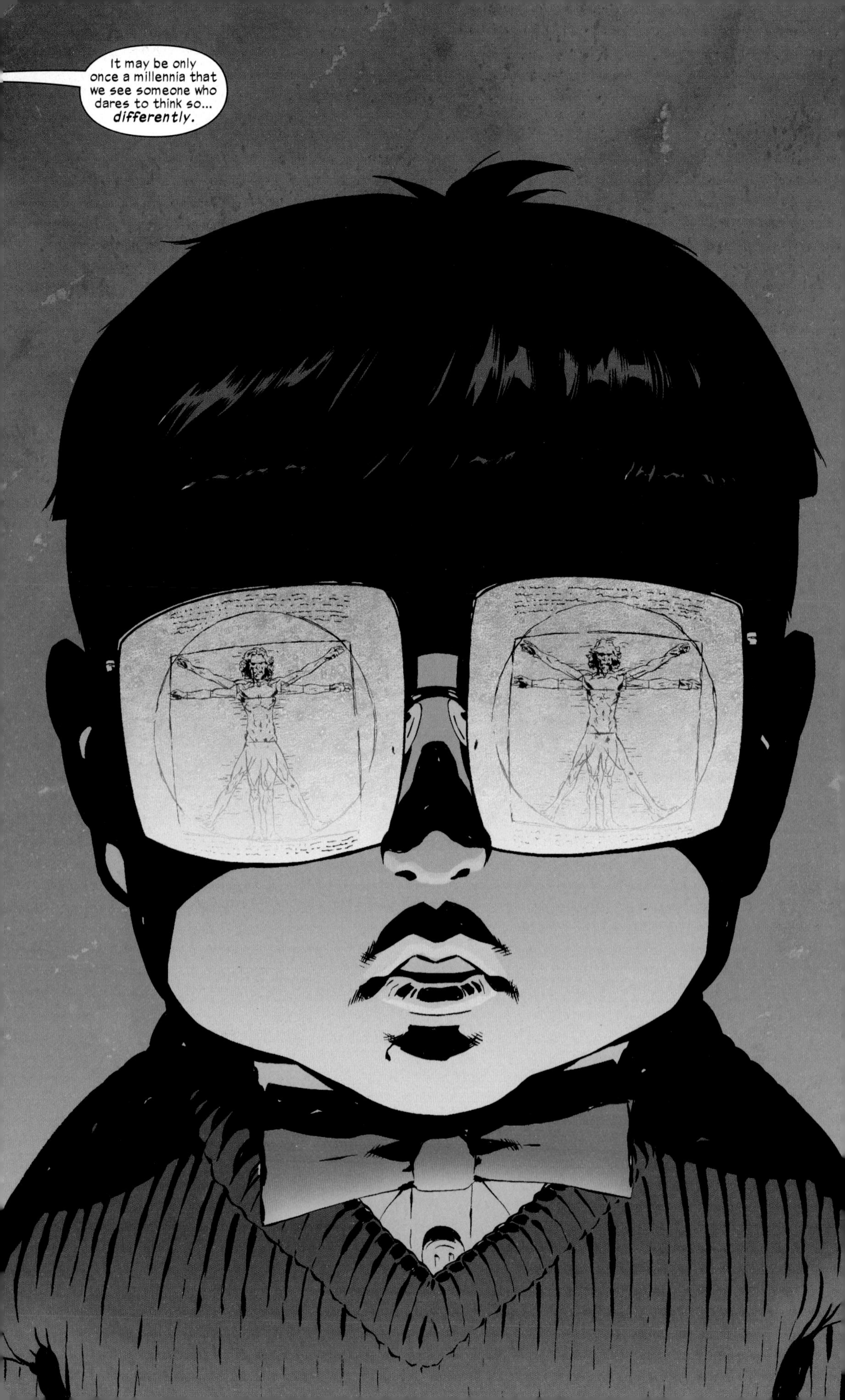
It may be only once a millennia that we see someone who dares to think so... *differently.*

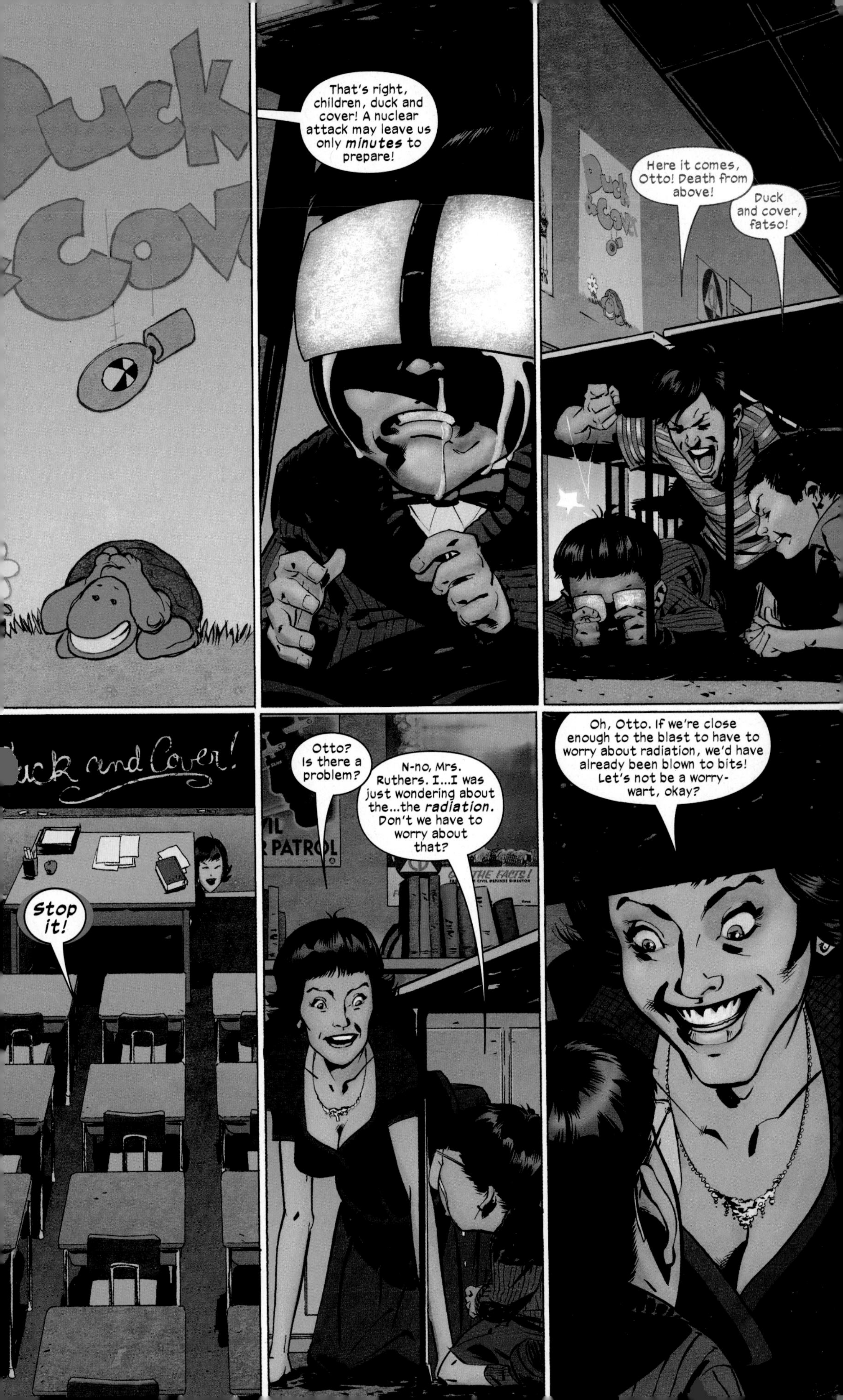
Duck & Cover
That's right, children, duck and cover! A nuclear attack may leave us only *minutes* to prepare!
Here it comes, Otto! Death from above!
Duck and cover, fatso!
Duck and Cover!
Stop it!
Otto? Is there a problem?
N-no, Mrs. Ruthers. I...I was just wondering about the...the *radiation*. Don't we have to worry about that?
Oh, Otto. If we're close enough to the blast to have to worry about radiation, we'd have already been blown to bits! Let's not be a worry-wart, okay?

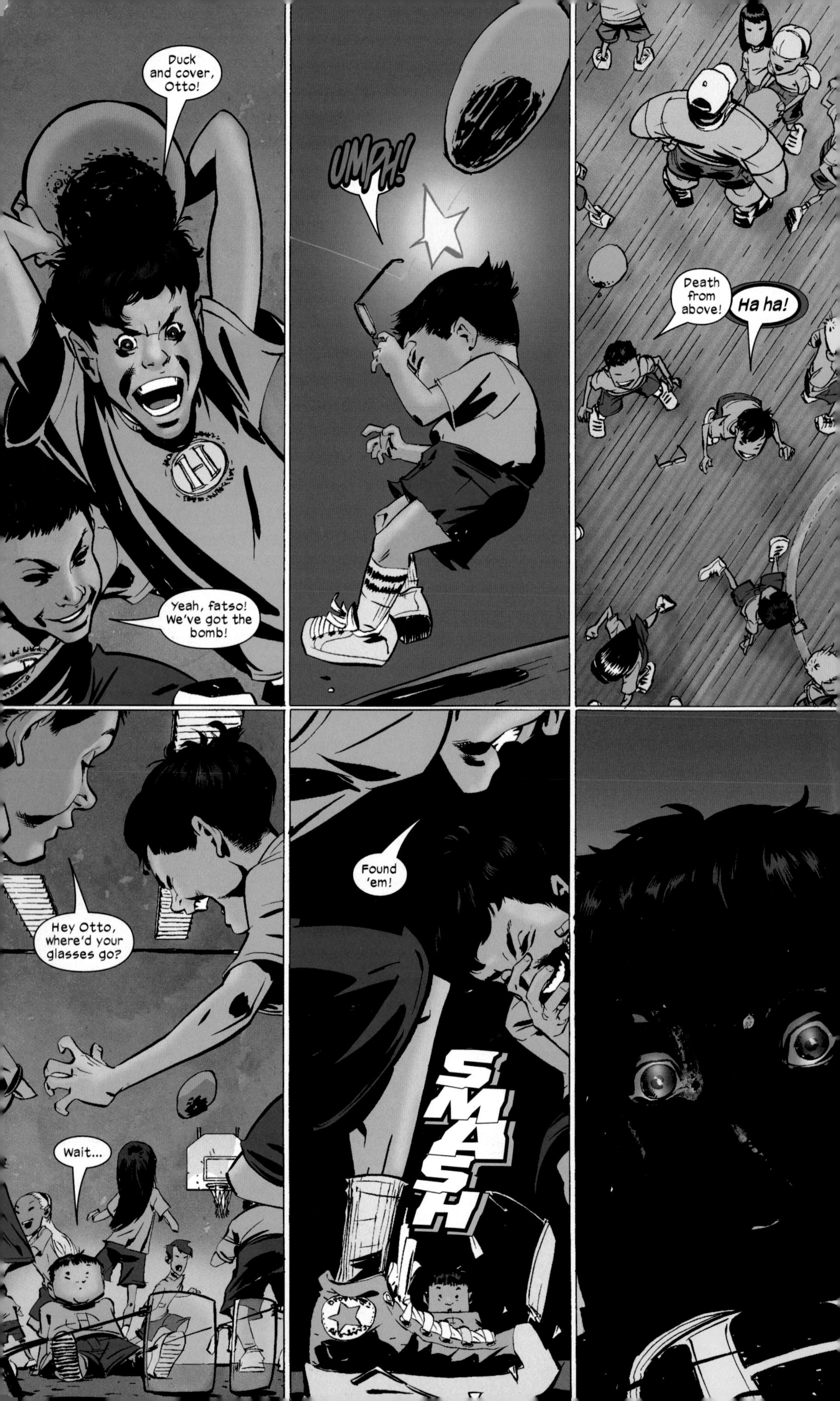

Duck and cover, Otto!
Yeah, fatso! We've got the bomb!
UMPH!
Death from above!
Ha ha!
Hey Otto, where'd your glasses go?
Wait...
Found 'em!
SMASH

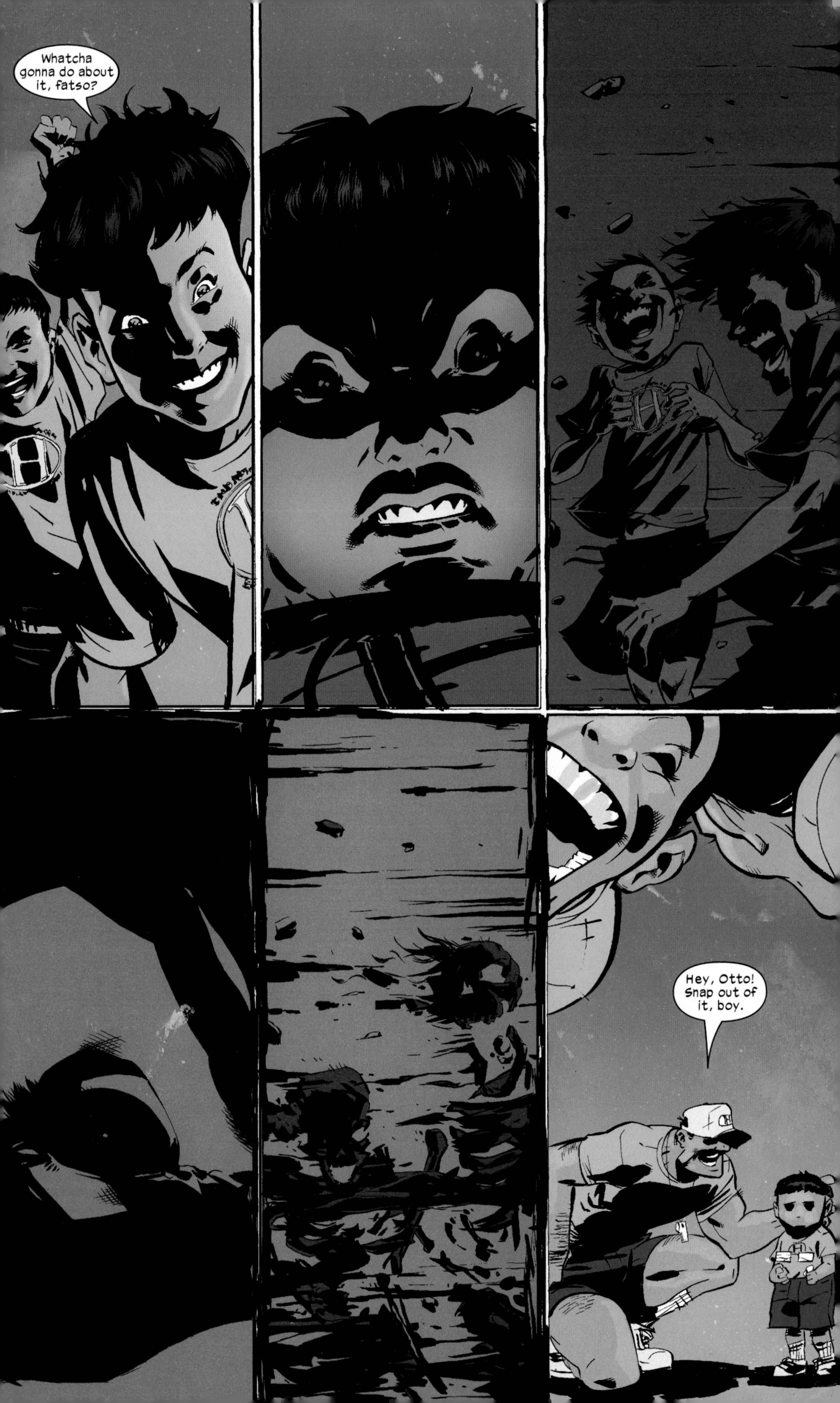
Whatcha gonna do about it, fatso?
Hey, Otto! Snap out of it, boy.

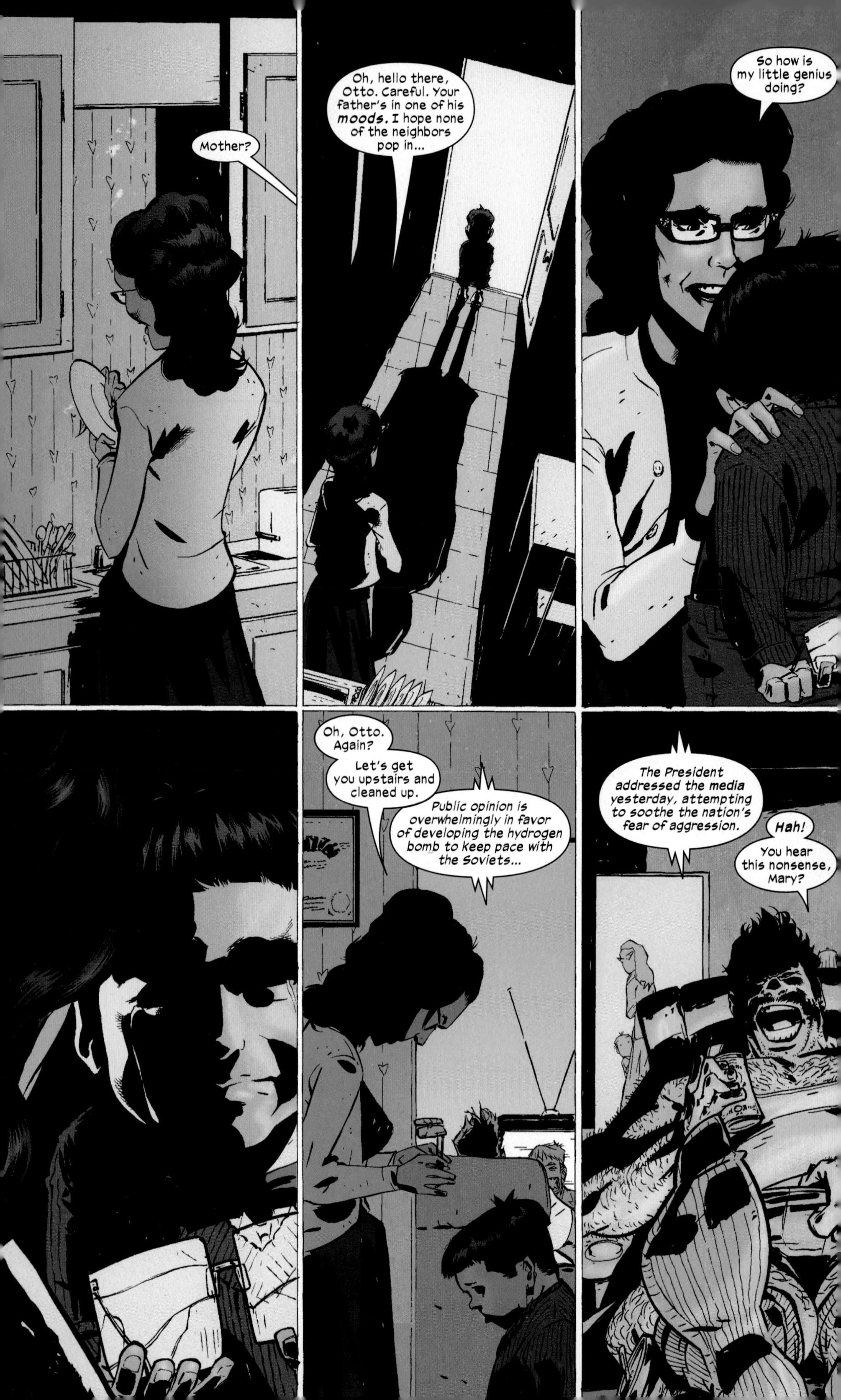
Mother?
Oh, hello there, Otto. Careful. Your father's in one of his moods. I hope none of the neighbors pop in...
So how is my little genius doing?
Oh, Otto. Again?
Let's get you upstairs and cleaned up.
Public opinion is overwhelmingly in favor of developing the hydrogen bomb to keep pace with the Soviets...
The President addressed the media yesterday, attempting to soothe the nation's fear of aggression.
Hah!
You hear this nonsense, Mary?

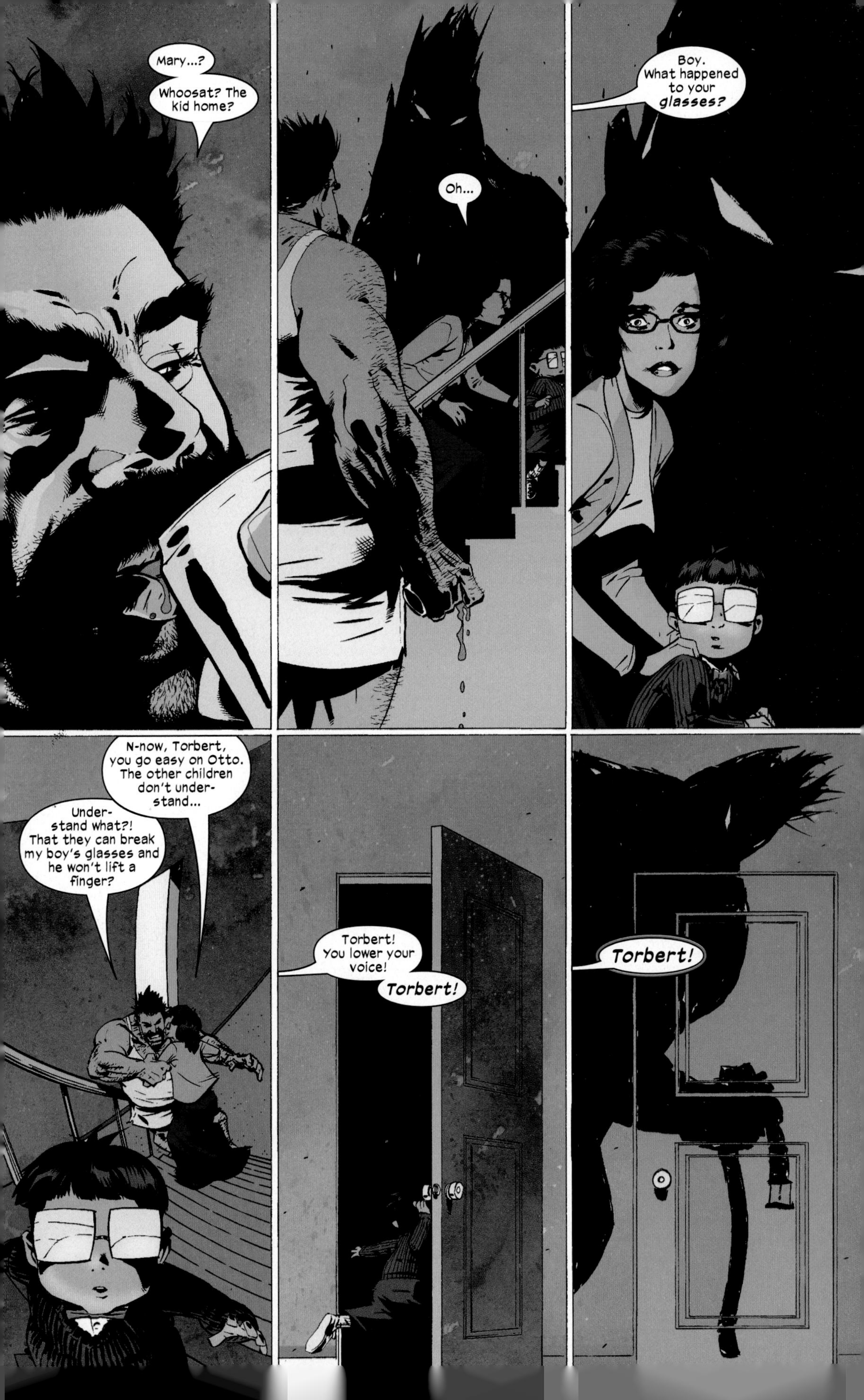

Mary...?
Whoosat? The kid home?
Oh...
Boy. What happened to your *glasses?*
N-now, Torbert, you go easy on Otto. The other children don't under-stand...
Under-stand what?! That they can break my boy's glasses and he won't lift a finger?
Torbert! You lower your voice!
Torbert!
Torbert!

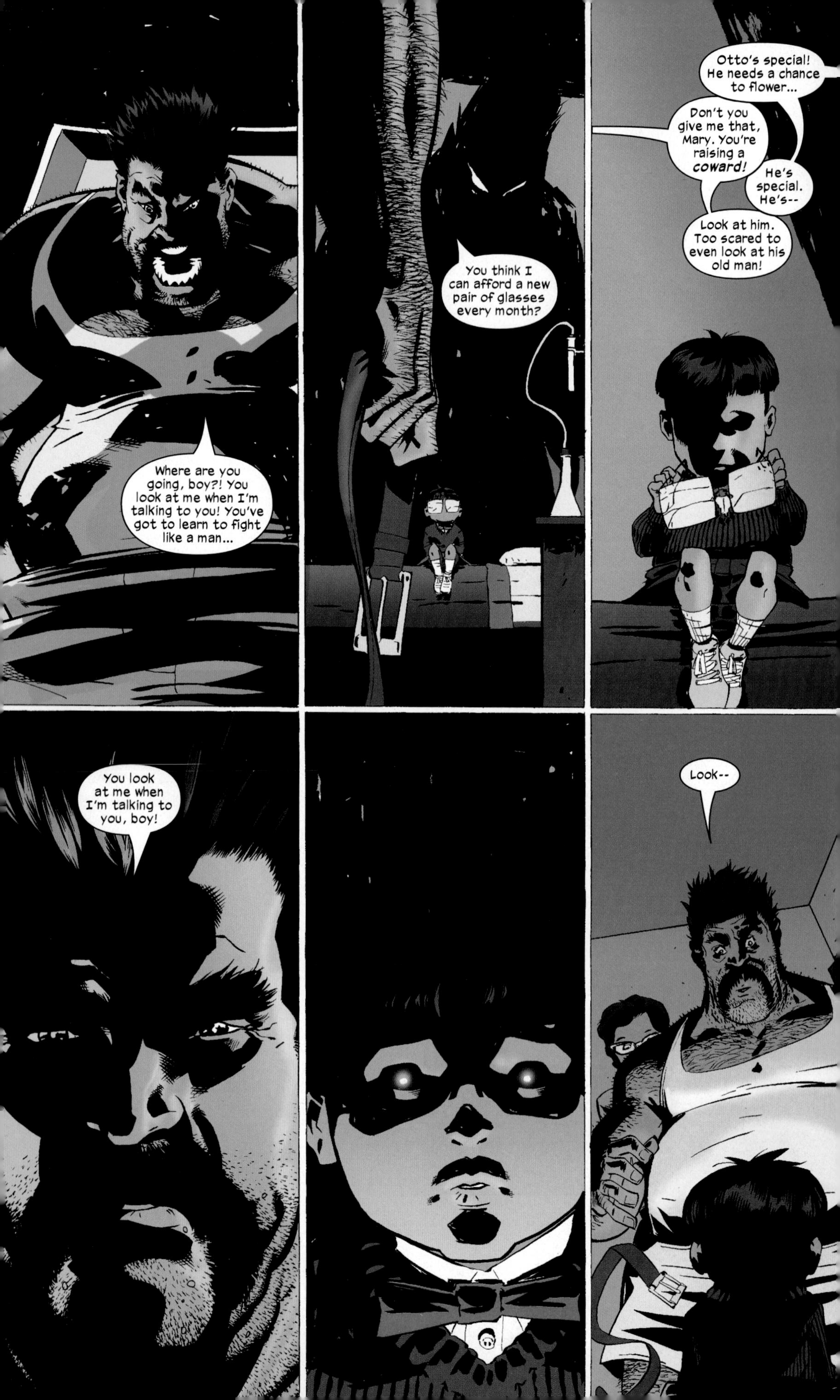
Where are you going, boy?! You look at me when I'm talking to you! You've got to learn to fight like a man...
You think I can afford a new pair of glasses every month?
Otto's special! He needs a chance to flower...
Don't you give me that, Mary. You're raising a *coward!*
He's special. He's--
Look at him. Too scared to even look at his old man!
You look at me when I'm talking to you, boy!
Look--

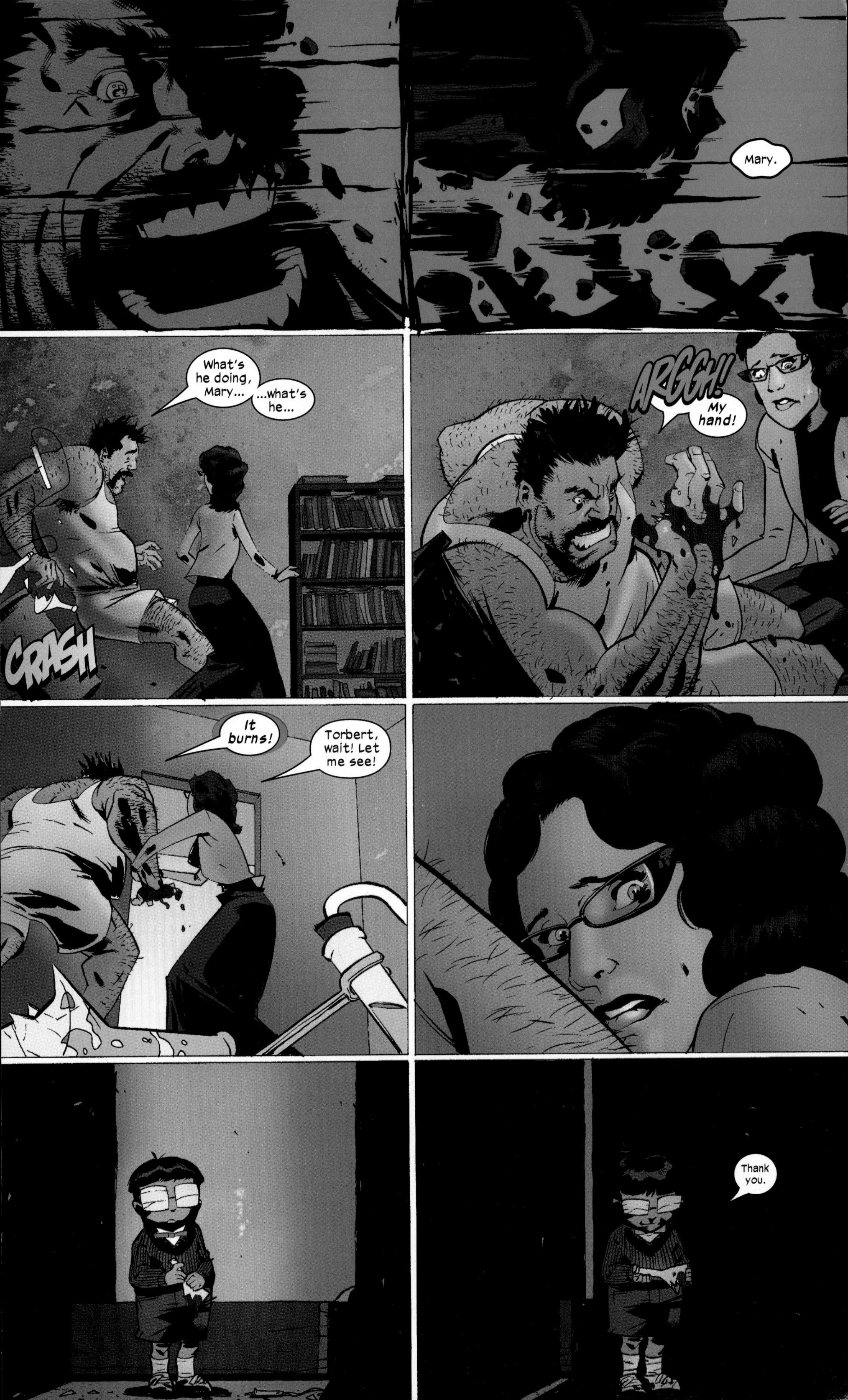
Mary.
What's he doing, Mary...
...what's he...
CRASH
ARGGH!
My hand!
It burns!
Torbert, wait! Let me see!
Thank you.

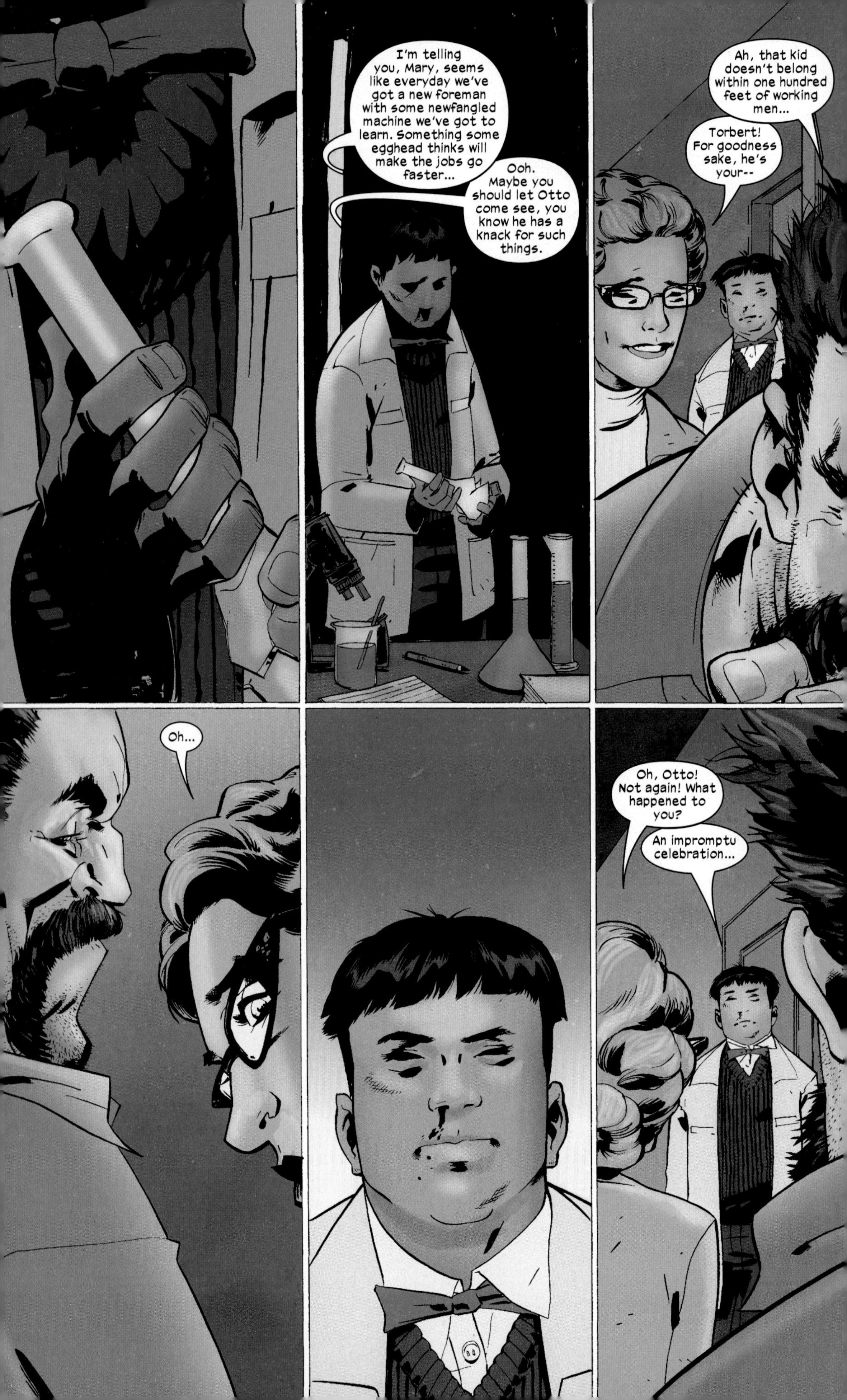
I'm telling you, Mary, seems like everyday we've got a new foreman with some newfangled machine we've got to learn. Something some egghead thinks will make the jobs go faster...
Ooh. Maybe you should let Otto come see, you know he has a knack for such things.
Ah, that kid doesn't belong within one hundred feet of working men...
Torbert! For goodness sake, he's your--
Oh...
Oh, Otto! Not again! What happened to you?
An impromptu celebration...

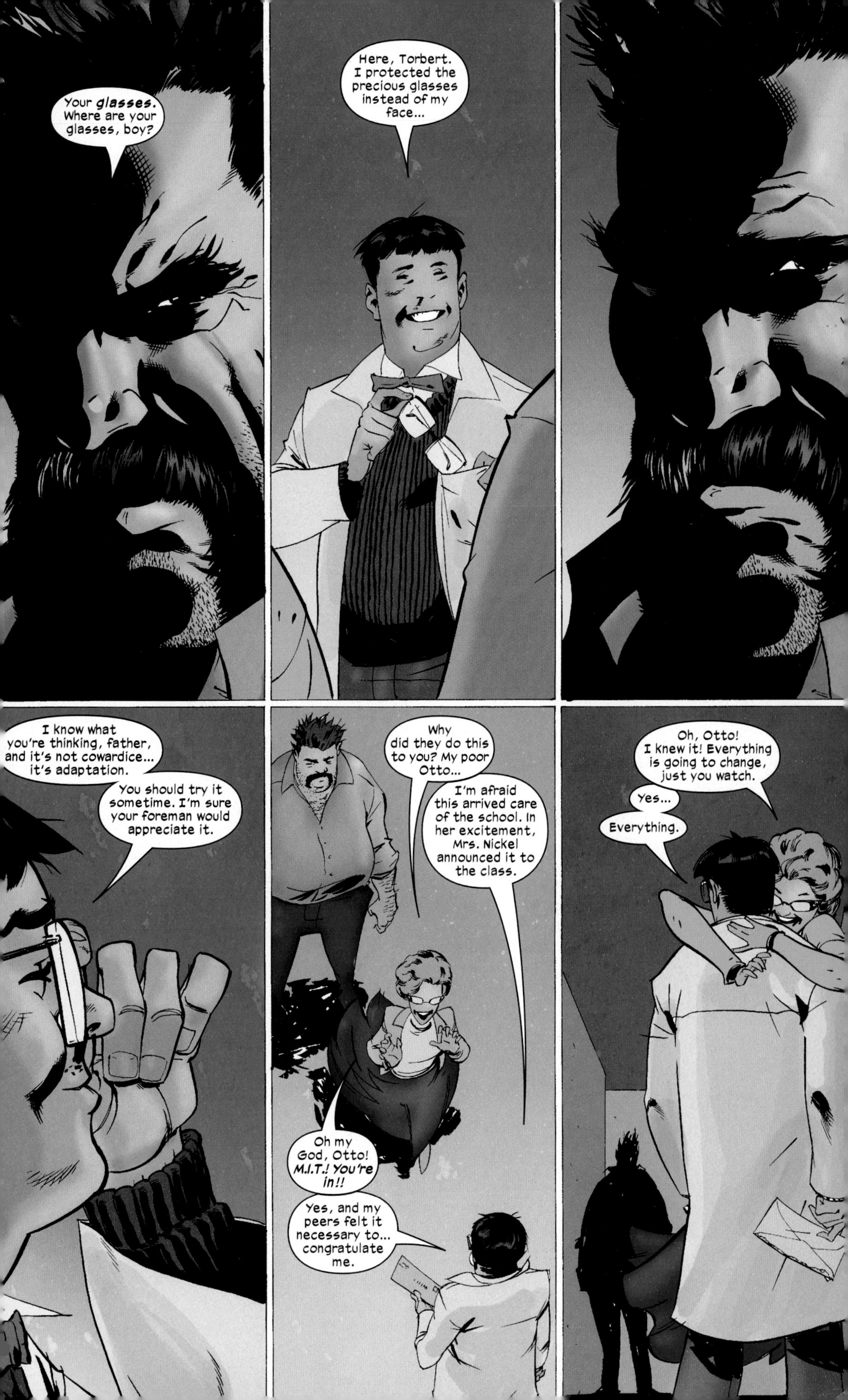

Your *glasses.* Where are your glasses, boy?
Here, Torbert. I protected the precious glasses instead of my face...
I know what you're thinking, father, and it's not cowardice... it's adaptation.
You should try it sometime. I'm sure your foreman would appreciate it.
Why did they do this to you? My poor Otto...
I'm afraid this arrived care of the school. In her excitement, Mrs. Nickel announced it to the class.
Oh my God, Otto! *M.I.T.! You're in!!*
Yes, and my peers felt it necessary to... congratulate me.
Oh, Otto! I knew it! Everything is going to change, just you watch.
Yes...
Everything.

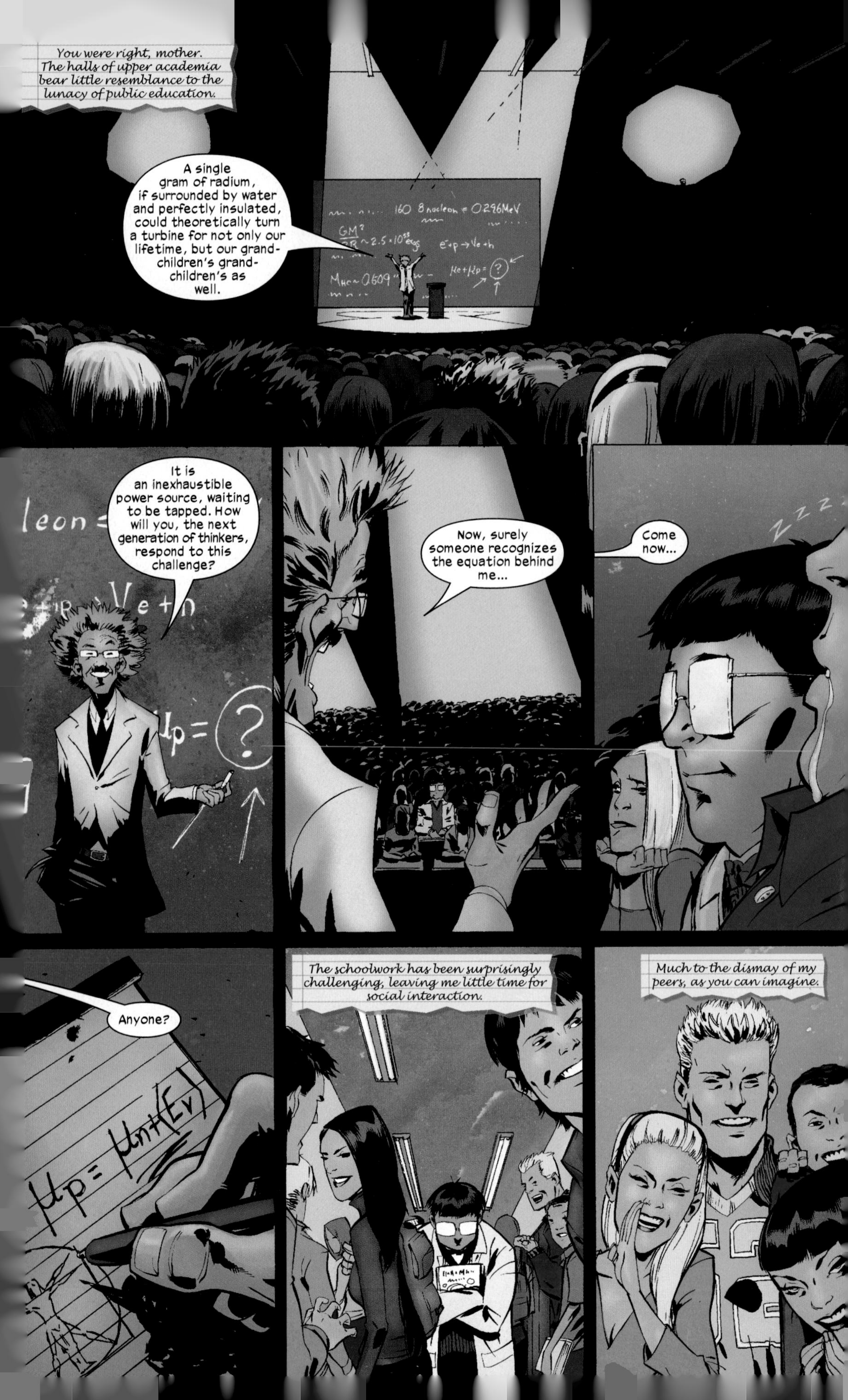
You were right, mother. The halls of upper academia bear little resemblance to the lunacy of public education.
A single gram of radium, if surrounded by water and perfectly insulated, could theoretically turn a turbine for not only our lifetime, but our grand-children's grand-children's as well.
It is an inexhaustible power source, waiting to be tapped. How will you, the next generation of thinkers, respond to this challenge?
Now, surely someone recognizes the equation behind me...
Come now...
Anyone?
The schoolwork has been surprisingly challenging, leaving me little time for social interaction.
Much to the dismay of my peers, as you can imagine.

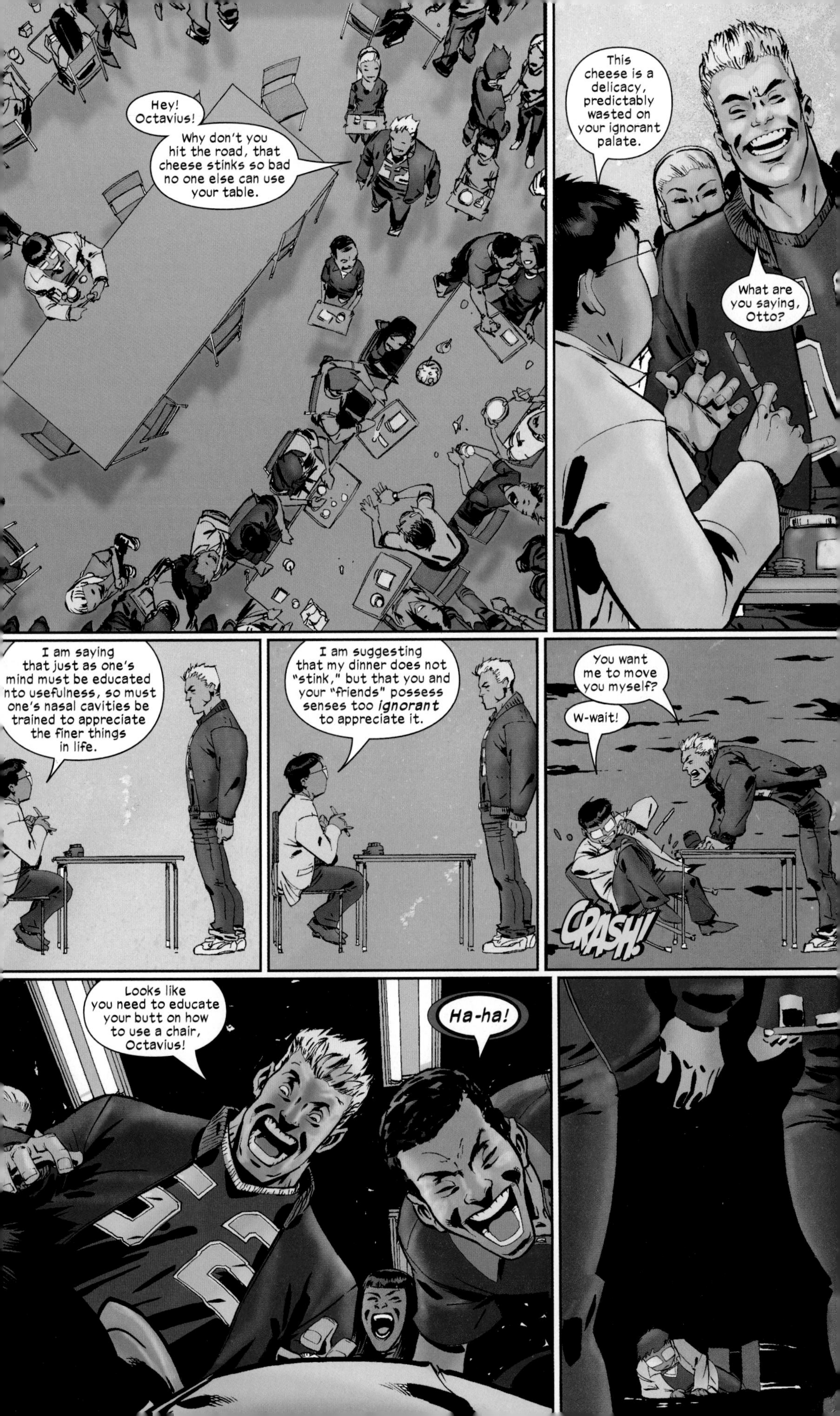
Hey! Octavius!
Why don't you hit the road, that cheese stinks so bad no one else can use your table.
This cheese is a delicacy, predictably wasted on your ignorant palate.
What are you saying, Otto?
I am saying that just as one's mind must be educated nto usefulness, so must one's nasal cavities be trained to appreciate the finer things in life.
I am suggesting that my dinner does not "stink," but that you and your "friends" possess senses too *ignorant* to appreciate it.
You want me to move you myself?
W-wait!
CRASH!
Looks like you need to educate your butt on how to use a chair, Octavius!
Ha-ha!

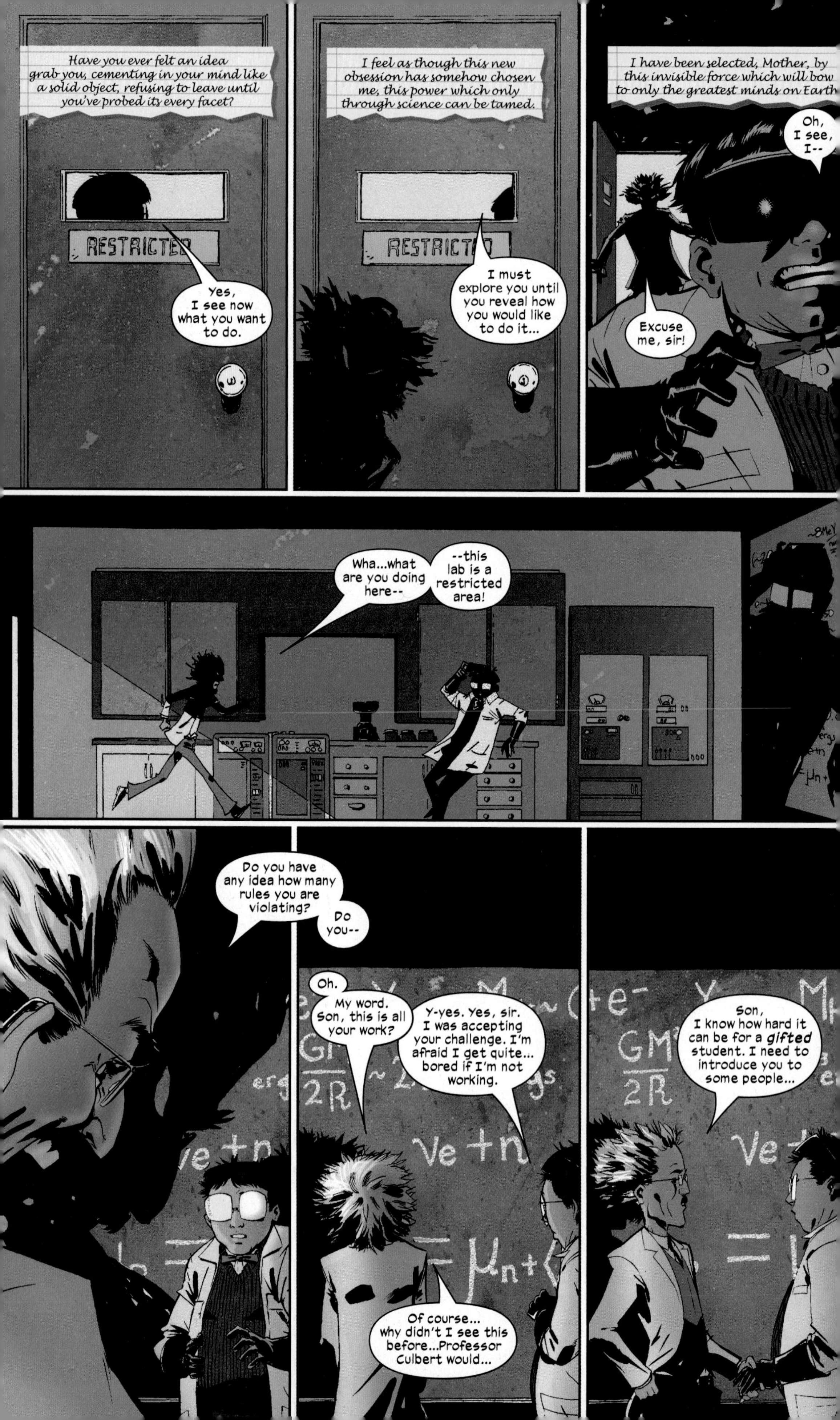
Have you ever felt an idea grab you, cementing in your mind like a solid object, refusing to leave until you've probed its every facet?
RESTRICTED
Yes, I see now what you want to do.
I feel as though this new obsession has somehow chosen me, this power which only through science can be tamed.
RESTRICTED
I must explore you until you reveal how you would like to do it...
I have been selected, Mother, by this invisible force which will bow to only the greatest minds on Earth
Oh, I see, I--
Excuse me, sir!
Wha...what are you doing here--
--this lab is a restricted area!
Do you have any idea how many rules you are violating?
Do you--
Oh.
My word. Son, this is all your work?
Y-yes. Yes, sir. I was accepting your challenge. I'm afraid I get quite... bored if I'm not working.
Of course... why didn't I see this before...Professor Culbert would...
Son, I know how hard it can be for a gifted student. I need to introduce you to some people...

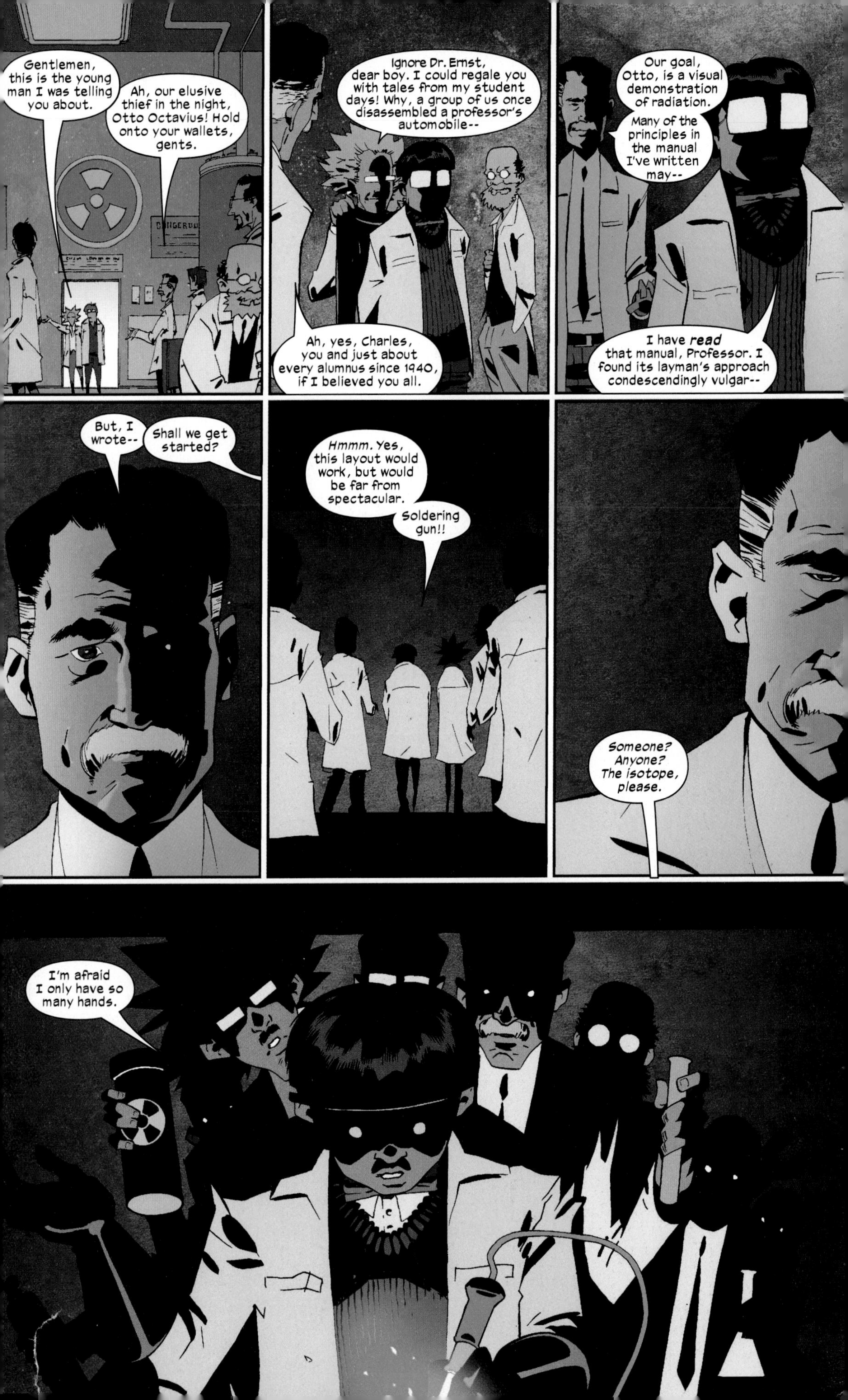
Gentlemen, this is the young man I was telling you about.
Ah, our elusive thief in the night, Otto Octavius! Hold onto your wallets, gents.
Ignore Dr. Ernst, dear boy. I could regale you with tales from my student days! Why, a group of us once disassembled a professor's automobile--
Ah, yes, Charles, you and just about every alumnus since 1940, if I believed you all.
Our goal, Otto, is a visual demonstration of radiation.
Many of the principles in the manual I've written may--
I have *read* that manual, Professor. I found its layman's approach condescendingly vulgar--
But, I wrote--
Shall we get started?
Hmmm. Yes, this layout would work, but would be far from spectacular.
Soldering gun!!
Someone? Anyone? The isotope, please.
I'm afraid I only have so many hands.

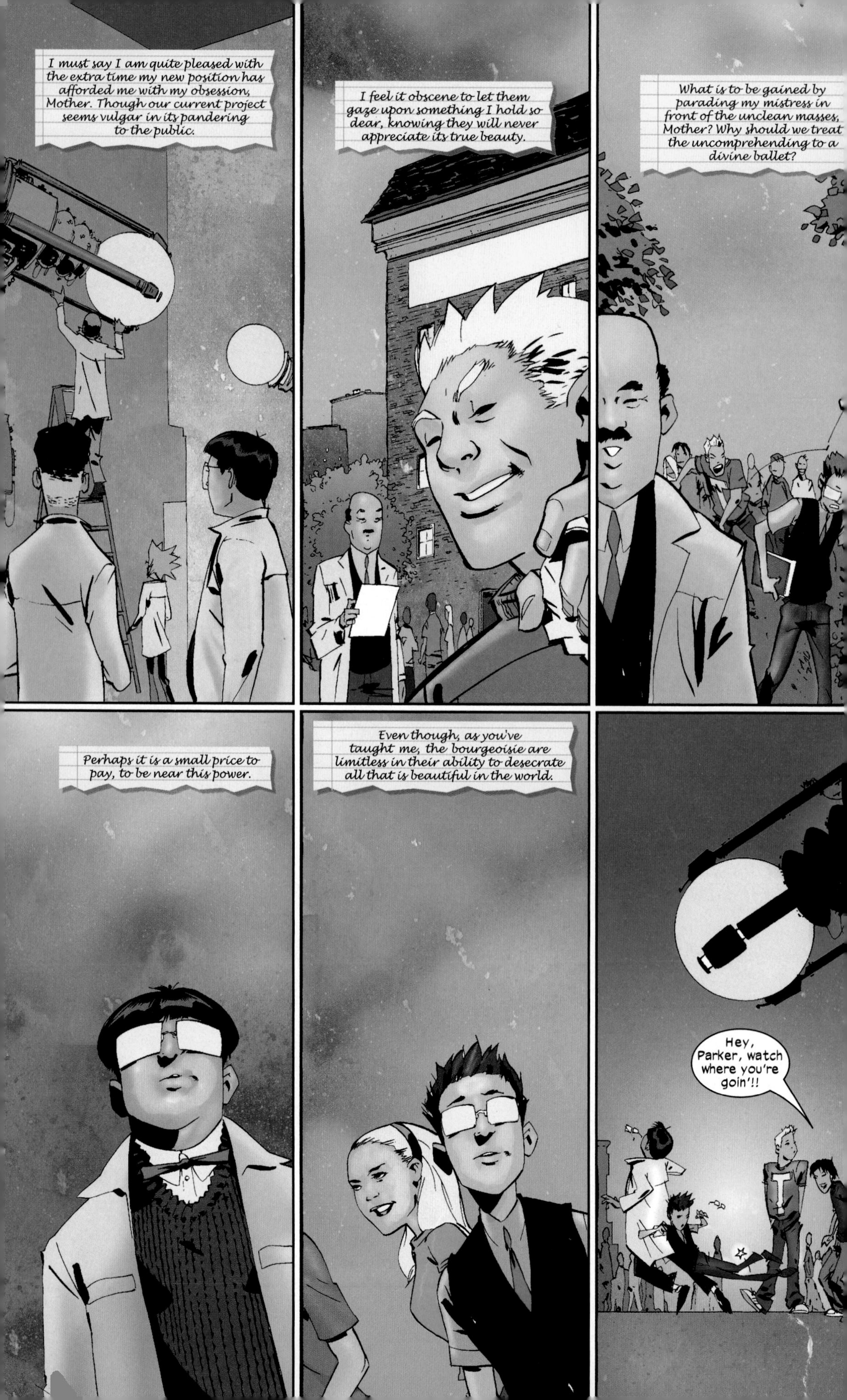
I must say I am quite pleased with the extra time my new position has afforded me with my obsession, Mother. Though our current project seems vulgar in its pandering to the public.
I feel it obscene to let them gaze upon something I hold so dear, knowing they will never appreciate its true beauty.
What is to be gained by parading my mistress in front of the unclean masses, Mother? Why should we treat the uncomprehending to a divine ballet?
Perhaps it is a small price to pay, to be near this power.
Even though, as you've taught me, the bourgeoisie are limitless in their ability to desecrate all that is beautiful in the world.
Hey, Parker, watch where you're goin'!!

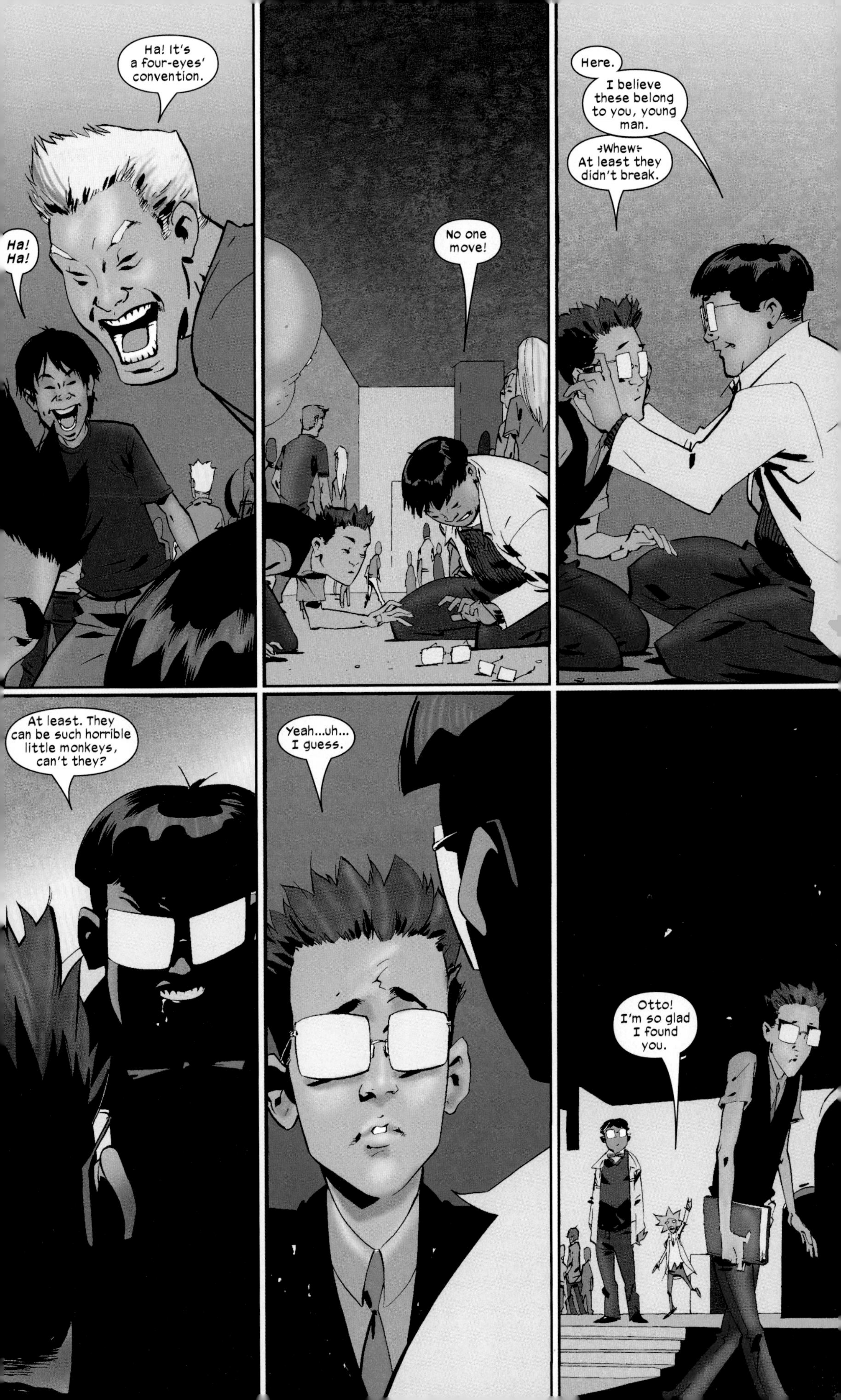
Ha! It's a four-eyes' convention.
Ha! Ha!
No one move!
Here.
I believe these belong to you, young man.
=Whew= At least they didn't break.
At least. They can be such horrible little monkeys, can't they?
Yeah...uh... I guess.
Otto! I'm so glad I found you.

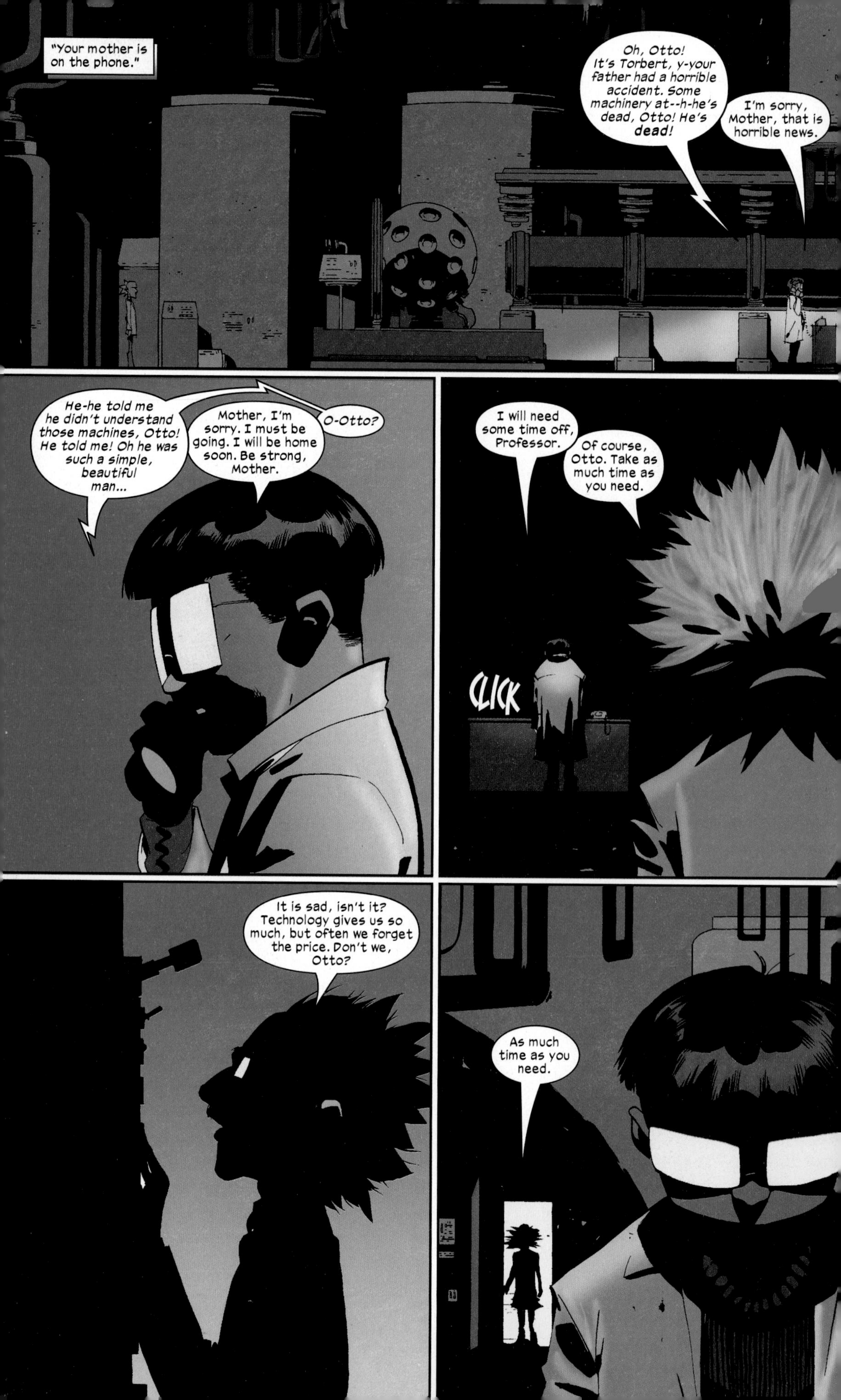
"Your mother is on the phone."
Oh, Otto! It's Torbert, y-your father had a horrible accident. Some machinery at--h-he's dead, Otto! He's dead!
I'm sorry, Mother, that is horrible news.
He-he told me he didn't understand those machines, Otto! He told me! Oh he was such a simple, beautiful man...
Mother, I'm sorry. I must be going. I will be home soon. Be strong, Mother.
O-Otto?
I will need some time off, Professor.
Of course, Otto. Take as much time as you need.
CLICK
It is sad, isn't it? Technology gives us so much, but often we forget the price. Don't we, Otto?
As much time as you need.

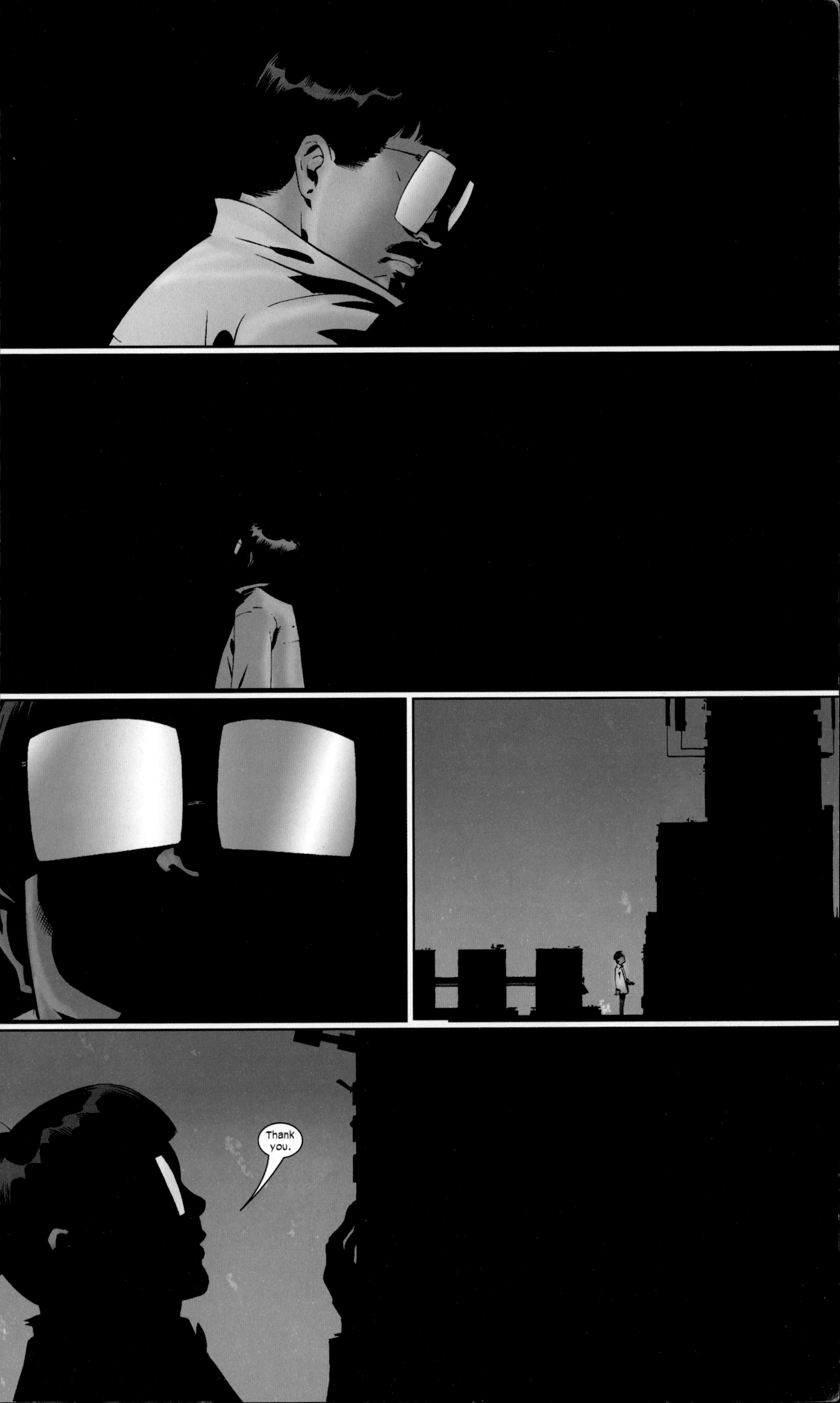
Thank you.

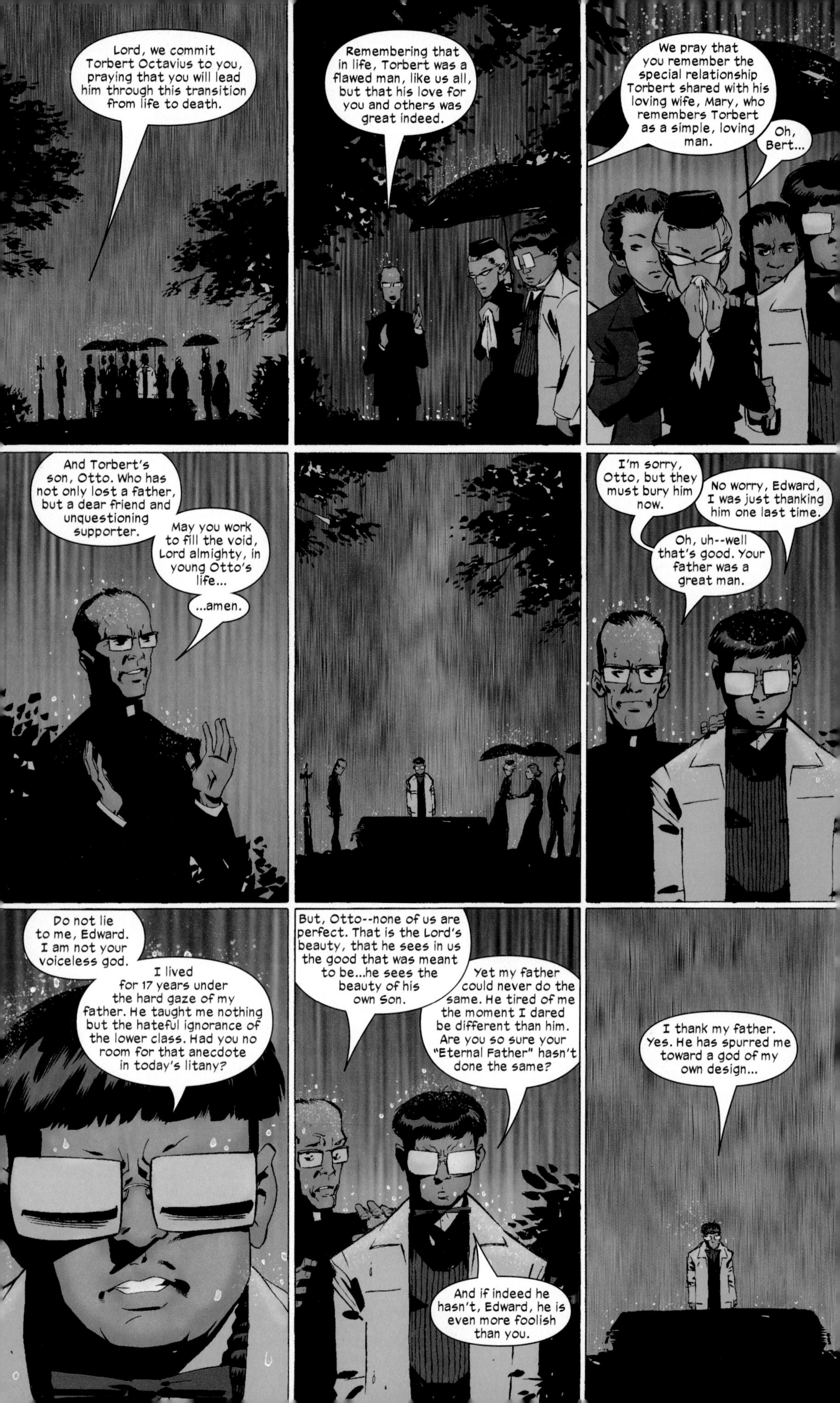

Lord, we commit Torbert Octavius to you, praying that you will lead him through this transition from life to death.
Remembering that in life, Torbert was a flawed man, like us all, but that his love for you and others was great indeed.
We pray that you remember the special relationship Torbert shared with his loving wife, Mary, who remembers Torbert as a simple, loving man.
Oh, Bert...
And Torbert's son, Otto. Who has not only lost a father, but a dear friend and unquestioning supporter.
May you work to fill the void, Lord almighty, in young Otto's life...
...amen.
I'm sorry, Otto, but they must bury him now.
No worry, Edward, I was just thanking him one last time.
Oh, uh--well that's good. Your father was a great man.
Do not lie to me, Edward. I am not your voiceless god.
I lived for 17 years under the hard gaze of my father. He taught me nothing but the hateful ignorance of the lower class. Had you no room for that anecdote in today's litany?
But, Otto--none of us are perfect. That is the Lord's beauty, that he sees in us the good that was meant to be...he sees the beauty of his own Son.
Yet my father could never do the same. He tired of me the moment I dared be different than him. Are you so sure your "Eternal Father" hasn't done the same?
And if indeed he hasn't, Edward, he is even more foolish than you.
I thank my father. Yes. He has spurred me toward a god of my own design...

Dean L.Q. Caswell

How is he holding up, then?

He's more determined than ever. Almost *frighteningly* driven.

And his grades?

Grades? Lawrence, I can assure you that applying academic scales to Otto's work would be a waste of time.

Our Defense Department liaison has been asking questions. I've seen it before. They're interested.

They *should* be. If he'd concentrate on the proofs to his theories, he'd be published already.

Well, why doesn't he?

The suggestion seems to irritate him. He wants his work accepted without question. He's prickly, but a genius, no doubt.

This campus is filled with geniuses, they'll need conventional proof that he's special.

I'm aware of that, Warren. But understand that Otto isn't building on the work of others. He has an almost artistic instinct when it comes to thermo-nuclear dynamics.

He is the perfect candidate for the advanced research program. I could almost guarantee the Department of Energy grant.

Hmm.

If our Department man bites...offer it to him.

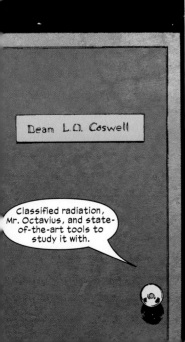

Dean L.Q. Caswell

Classified radiation, Mr. Octavius, and state-of-the-art tools to study it with.

Not to mention a doctorate degree in half the time.

Beautiful...

But my-my mother. She has no one to take care of her, now. I can't leave--

Bring her along, Otto! There is a generous stipend...

You'd be working for Uncle Sam, after all.

I'll take it. Of course.

Welcome to the good fight, young man.

Have the papers brought in immediately.

Yes, sir!

Enjoy your last minutes as a student, Otto. Your future is right around the corner.

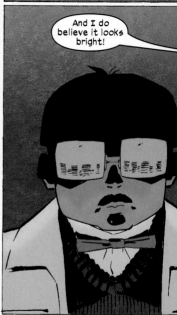
And I do believe it looks bright!

Yes...

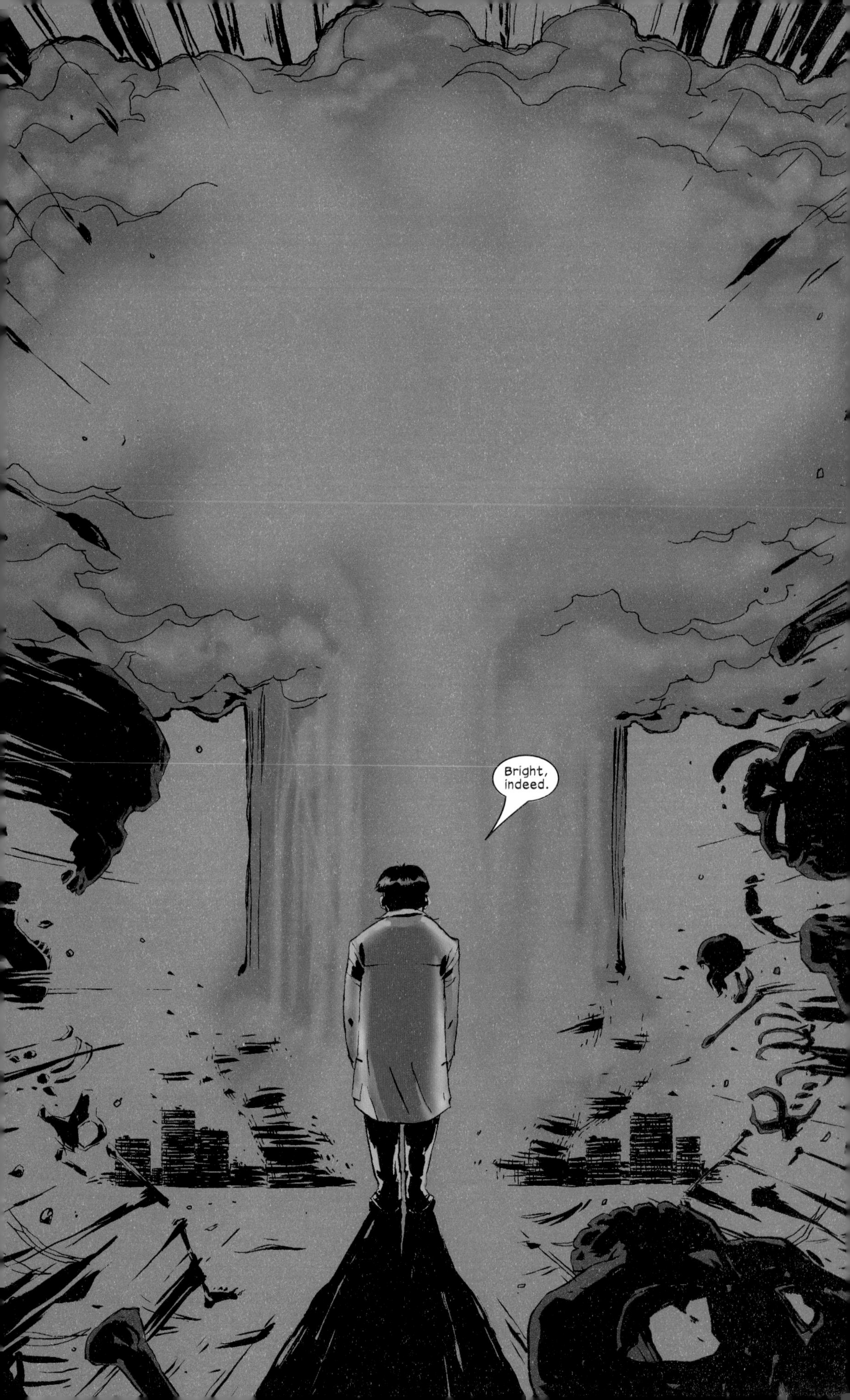
Bright, indeed.

2

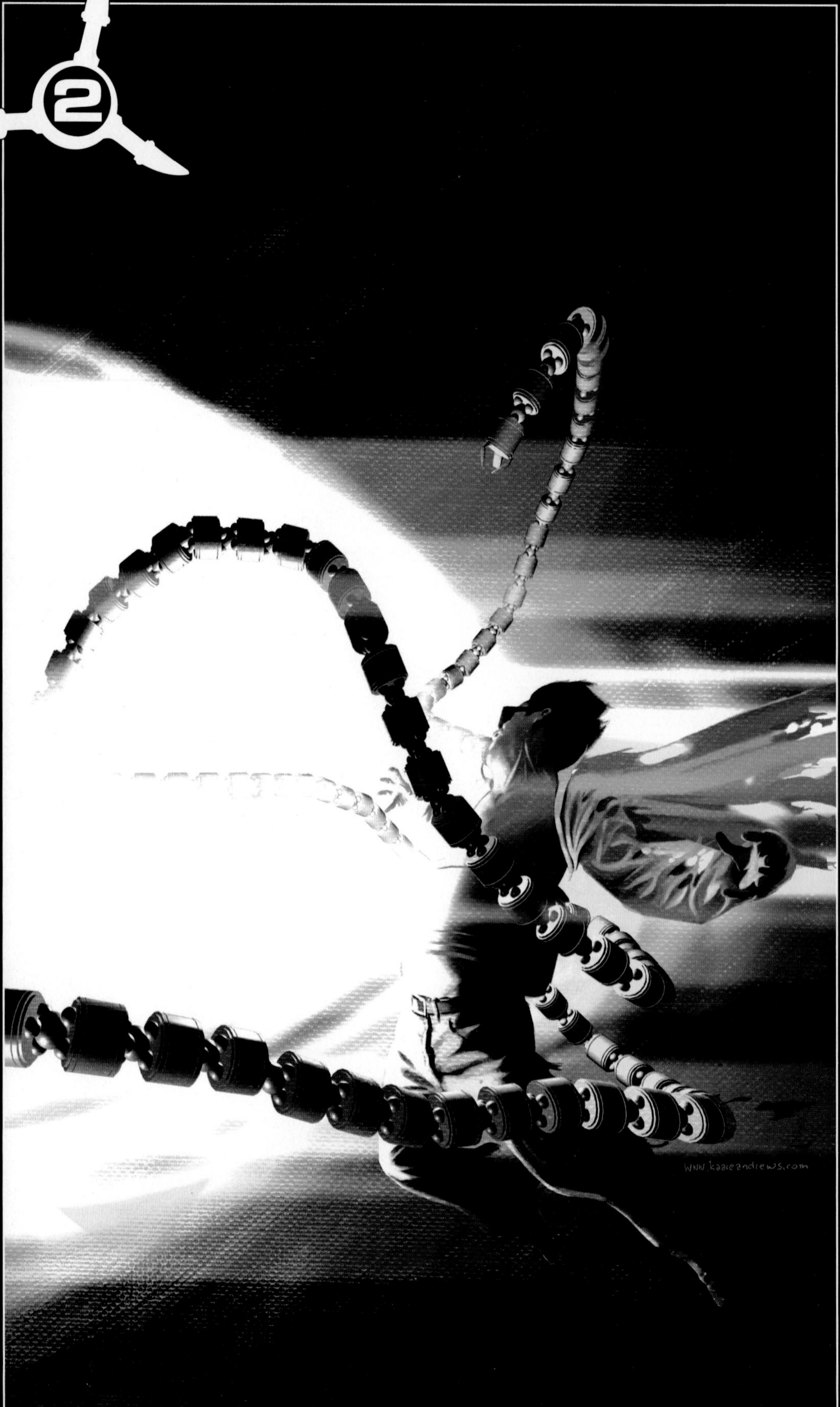
www.kaareandrews.com

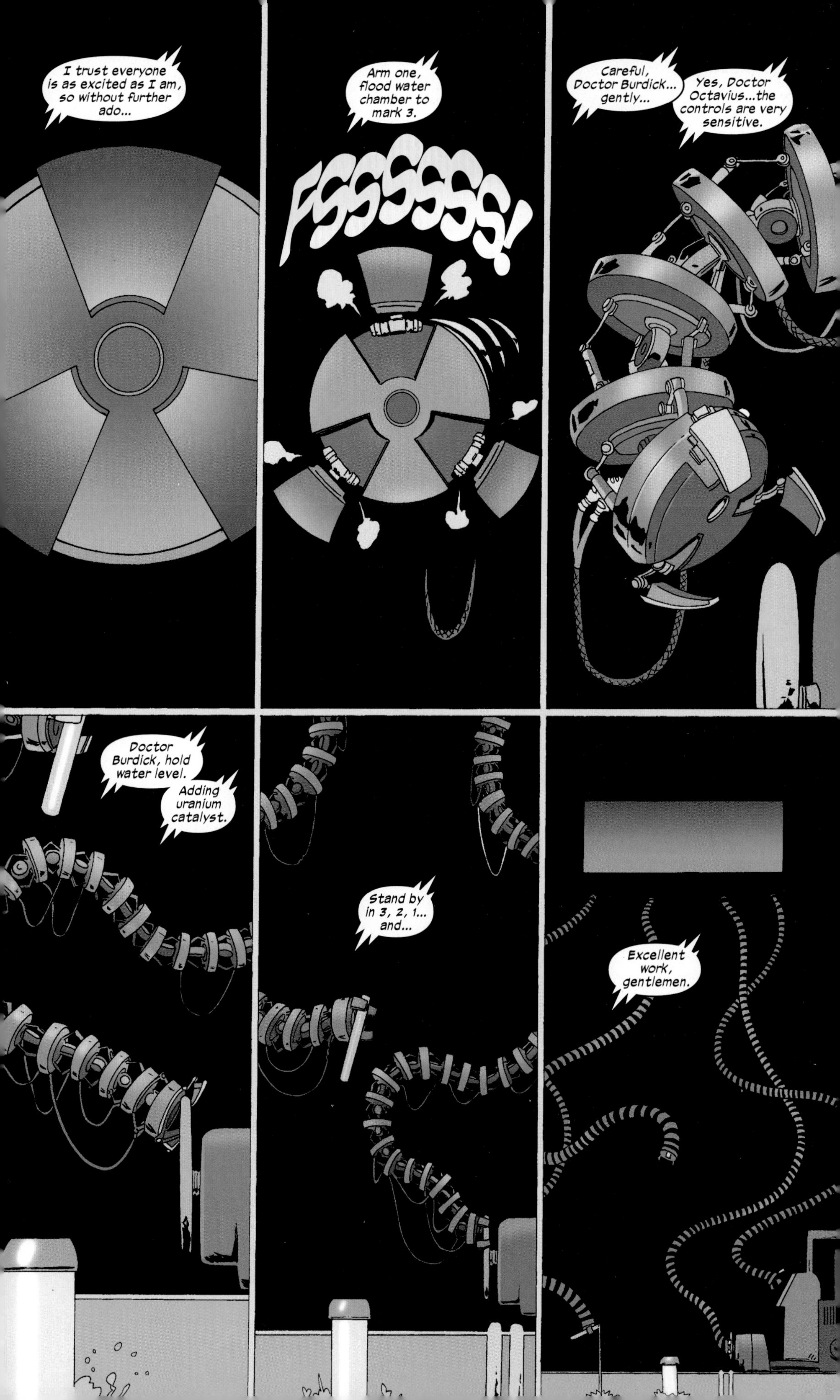
I trust everyone is as excited as I am, so without further ado...
Arm one, flood water chamber to mark 3.
FSSSSSS!
Careful, Doctor Burdick... gently...
Yes, Doctor Octavius...the controls are very sensitive.
Doctor Burdick, hold water level.
Adding uranium catalyst.
Stand by in 3, 2, 1... and...
Excellent work, gentlemen.

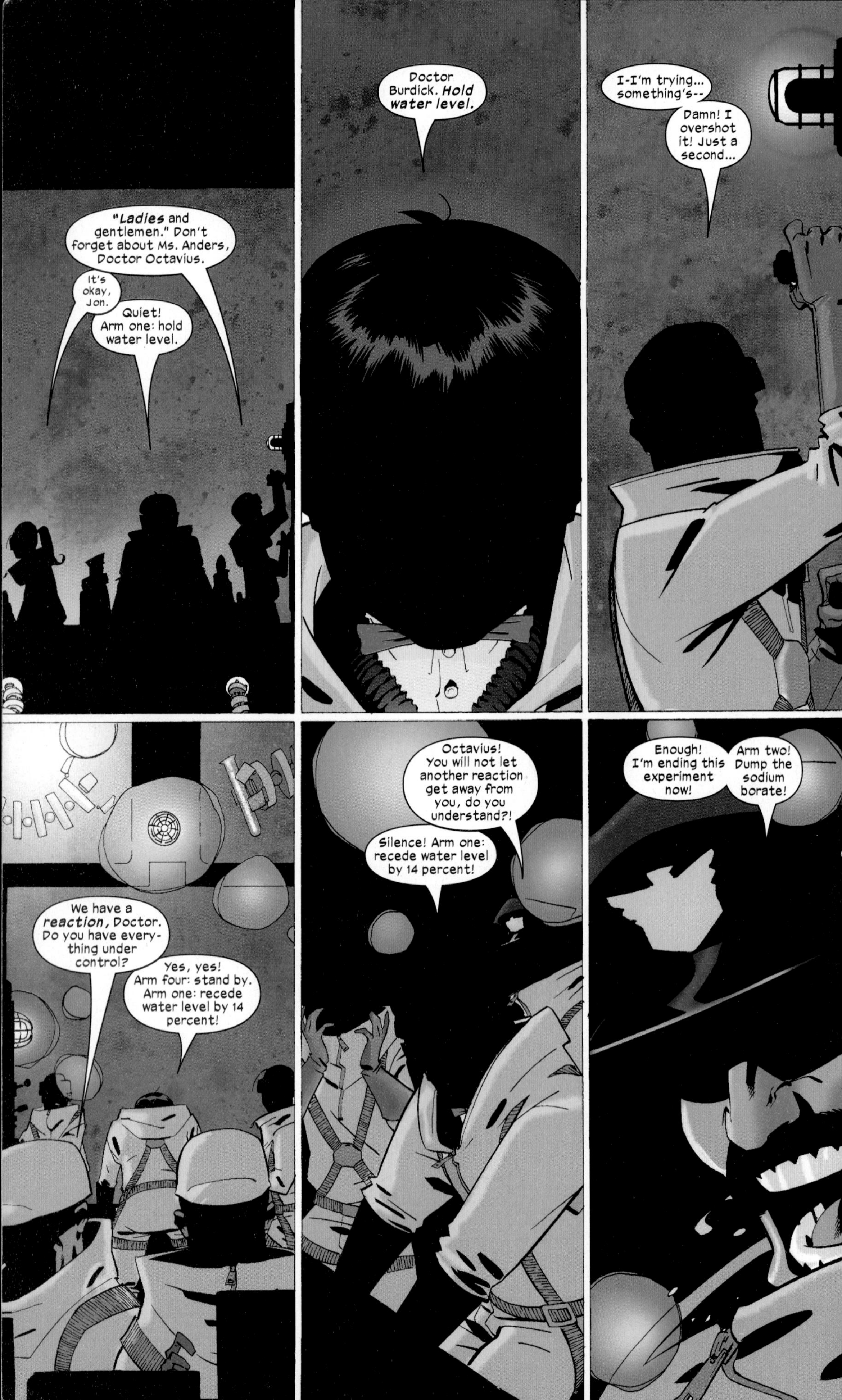
"*Ladies* and gentlemen." Don't forget about Ms. Anders, Doctor Octavius.
It's okay, Jon.
Quiet! Arm one: hold water level.
Doctor Burdick. *Hold water level.*
I-I'm trying... something's--
Damn! I overshot it! Just a second...
We have a *reaction,* Doctor. Do you have every-thing under control?
Yes, yes! Arm four: stand by. Arm one: recede water level by 14 percent!
Octavius! You will not let another reaction get away from you, do you understand?!
Silence! Arm one: recede water level by 14 percent!
Enough! I'm ending this experiment now!
Arm two! Dump the sodium borate!

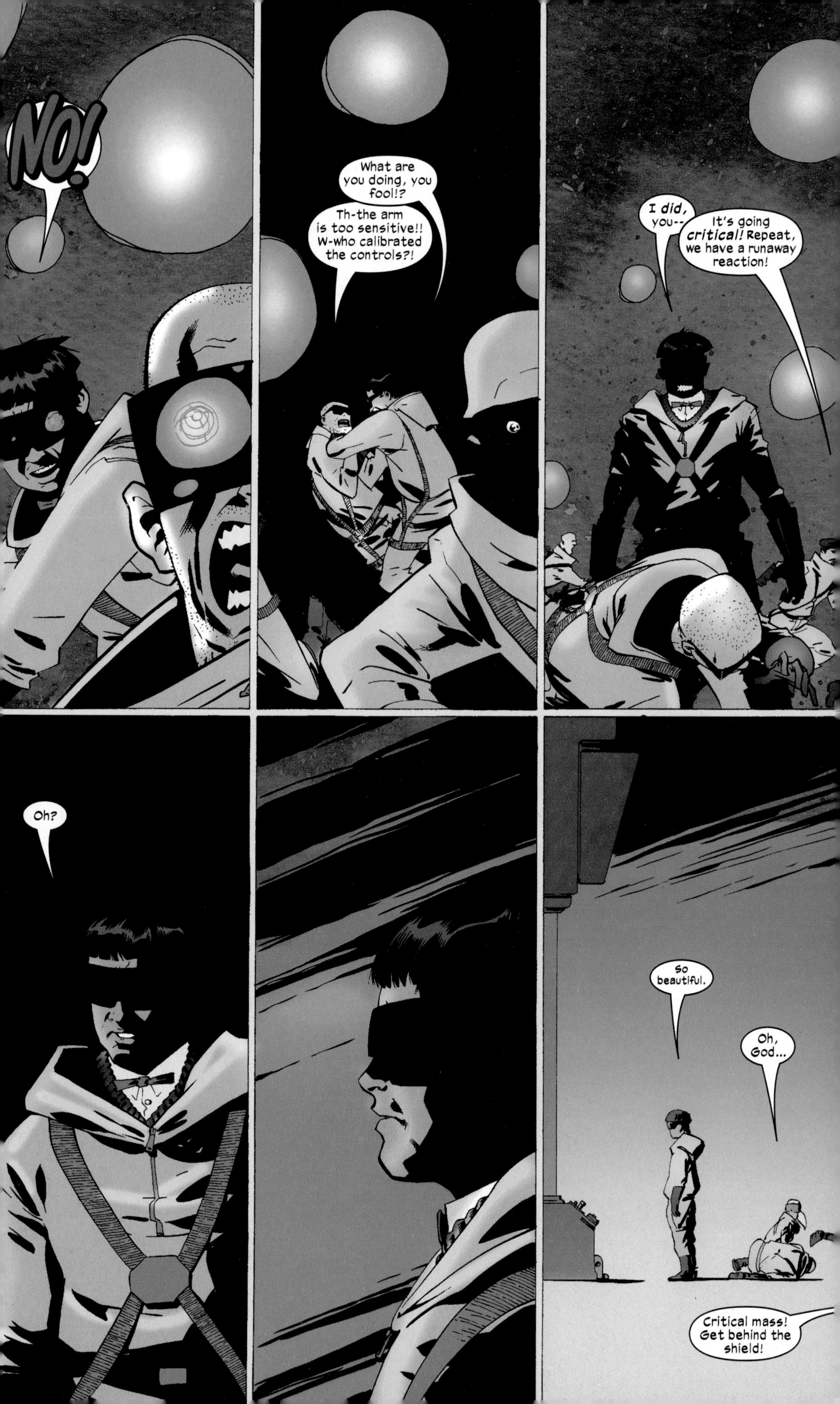
NO!
What are you doing, you fool!?
Th-the arm is too sensitive!! W-who calibrated the controls?!
I did, you--
It's going critical! Repeat, we have a runaway reaction!
Oh?
So beautiful.
Oh, God...
Critical mass! Get behind the shield!

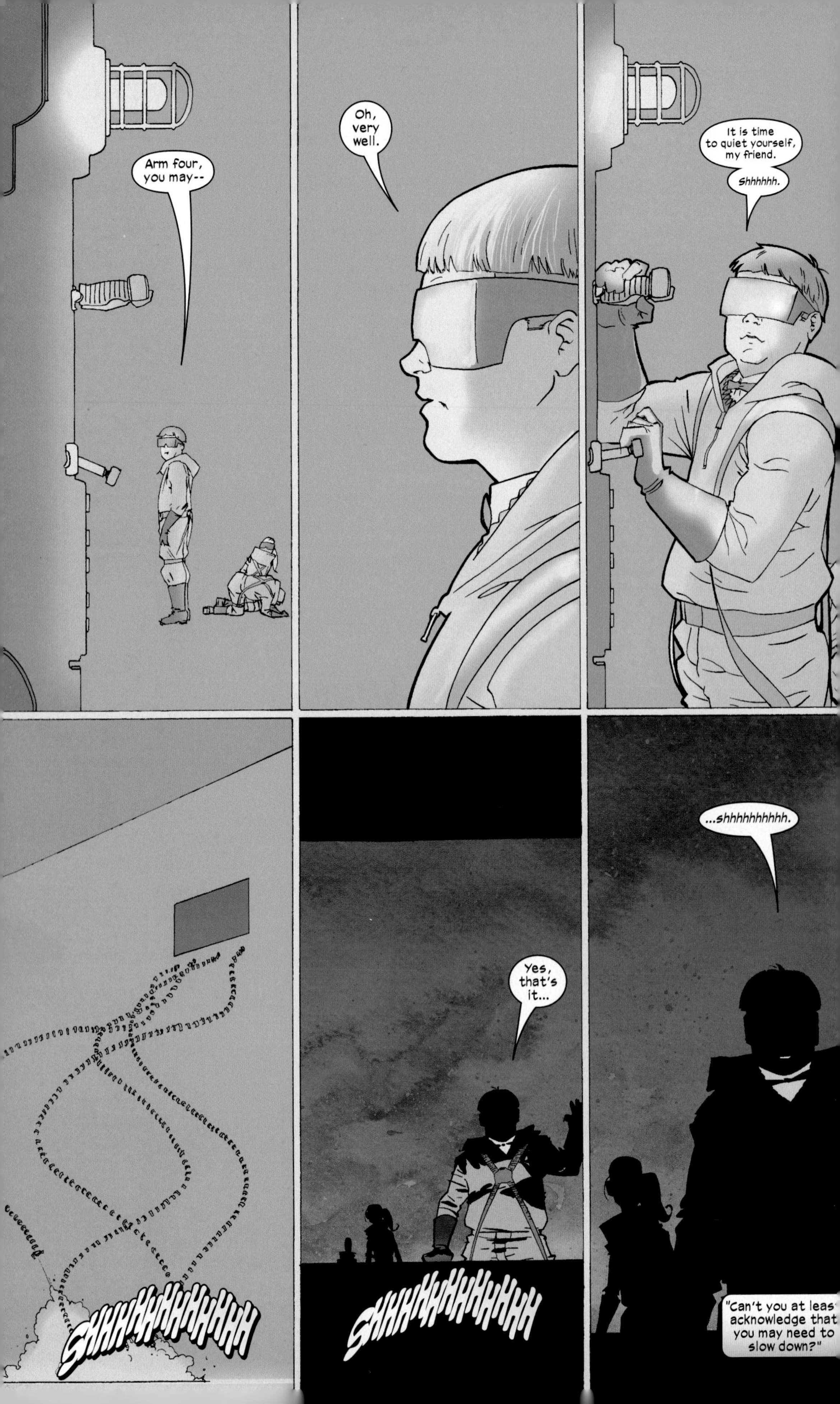
Arm four, you may--
Oh, very well.
It is time to quiet yourself, my friend.
Shhhhhh.
SHHHHHHHHHHHH
Yes, that's it...
SHHHHHHHHHHHH
...shhhhhhhhhh.
"Can't you at leas acknowledge that you may need to slow down?"

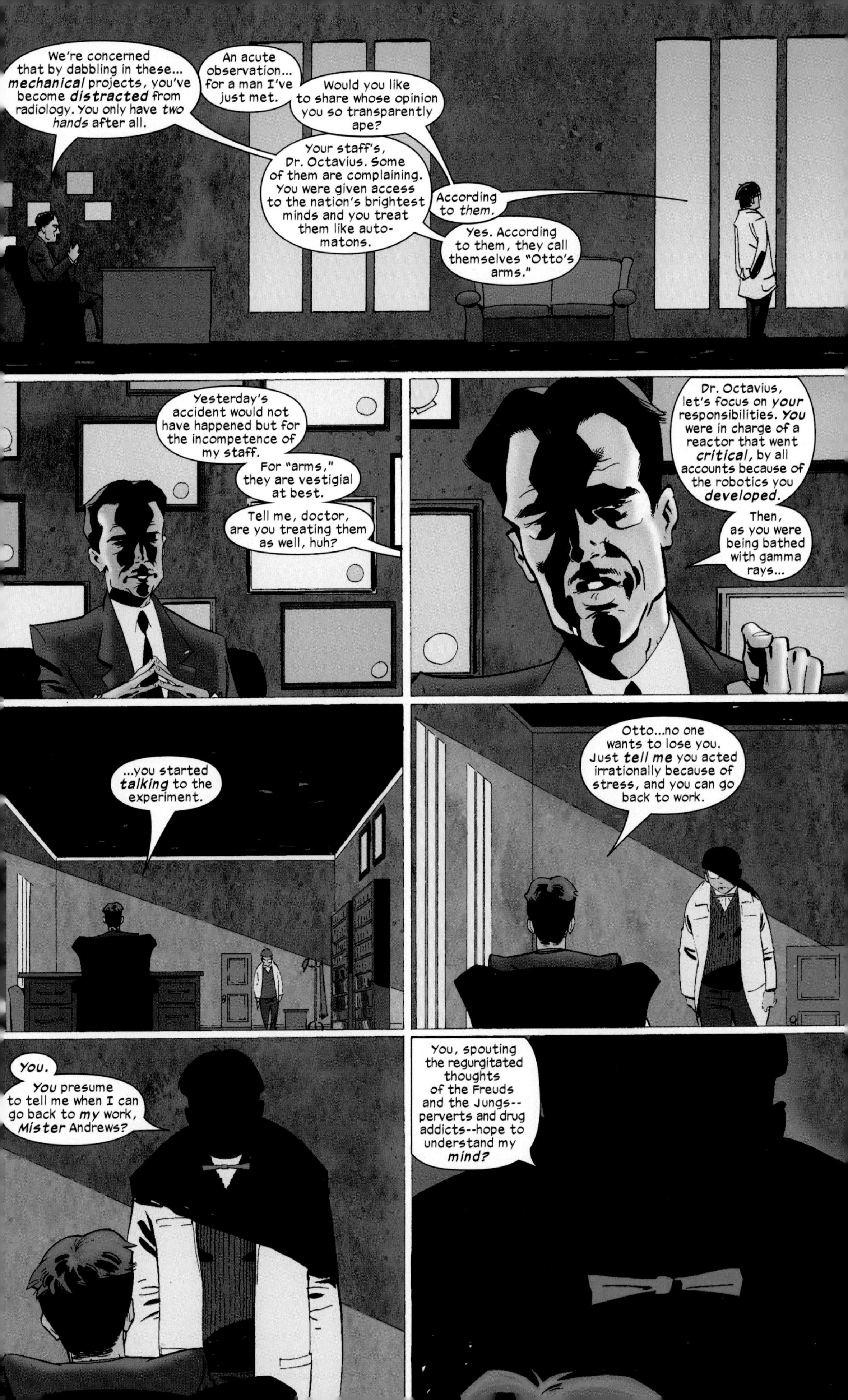
We're concerned that by dabbling in these... mechanical projects, you've become distracted from radiology. You only have two hands after all.
An acute observation... for a man I've just met.
Would you like to share whose opinion you so transparently ape?
Your staff's, Dr. Octavius. Some of them are complaining. You were given access to the nation's brightest minds and you treat them like automatons.
According to them.
Yes. According to them, they call themselves "Otto's arms."
Yesterday's accident would not have happened but for the incompetence of my staff.
For "arms," they are vestigial at best.
Tell me, doctor, are you treating them as well, huh?
Dr. Octavius, let's focus on your responsibilities. You were in charge of a reactor that went critical, by all accounts because of the robotics you developed.
Then, as you were being bathed with gamma rays...
...you started talking to the experiment.
Otto...no one wants to lose you. Just tell me you acted irrationally because of stress, and you can go back to work.
You.
You presume to tell me when I can go back to my work, Mister Andrews?
You, spouting the regurgitated thoughts of the Freuds and the Jungs--perverts and drug addicts--hope to understand my mind?

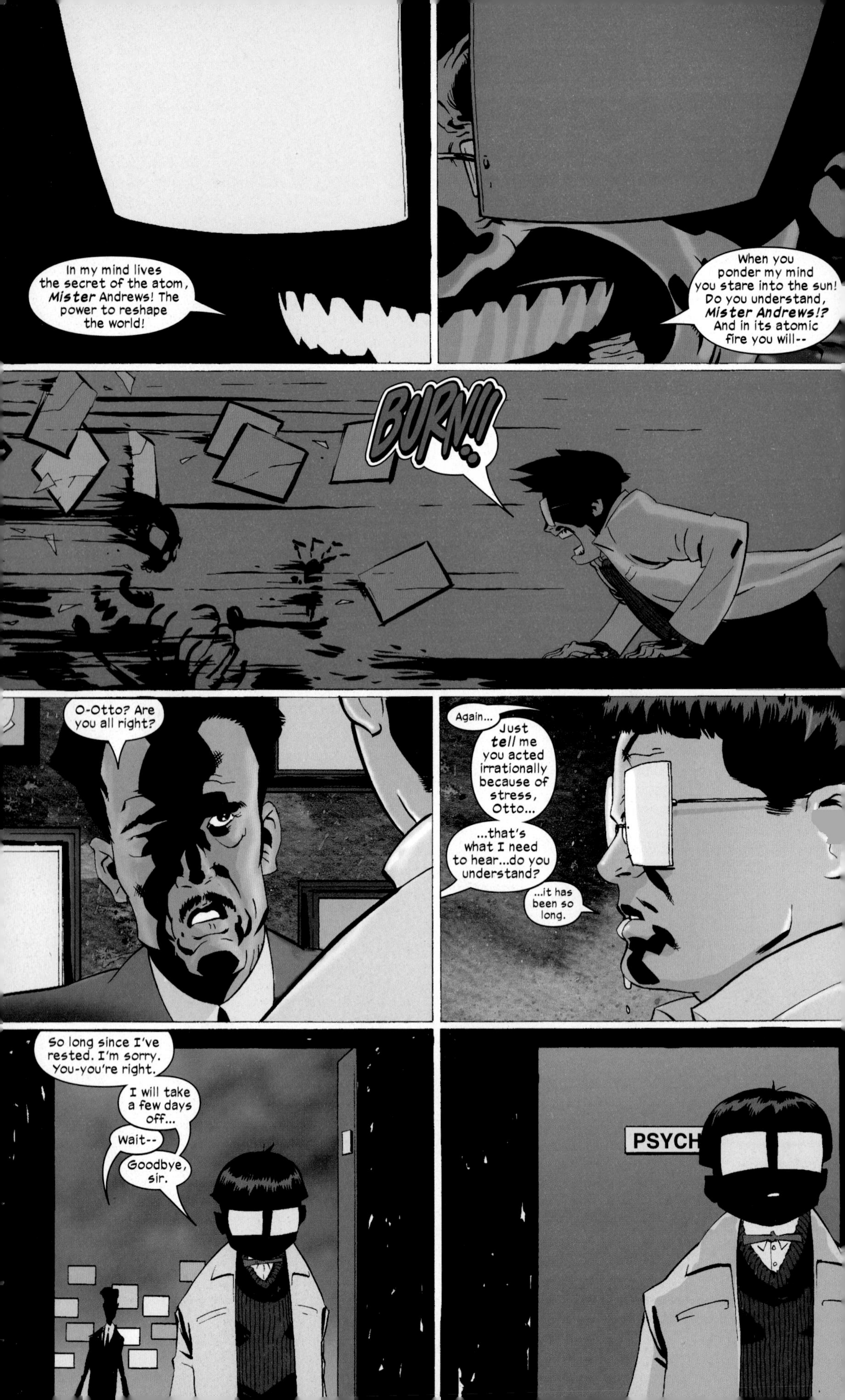
In my mind lives the secret of the atom, *Mister* Andrews! The power to reshape the world!
When you ponder my mind you stare into the sun! Do you understand, ***Mister Andrews!?*** And in its atomic fire you will--
BURN!!!
O-Otto? Are you all right?
Again...
Just *tell* me you acted irrationally because of stress, Otto...
...that's what I need to hear...do you understand?
...it has been so long.
So long since I've rested. I'm sorry. You-you're right.
I will take a few days off...
Wait--
Goodbye, sir.
PSYCH

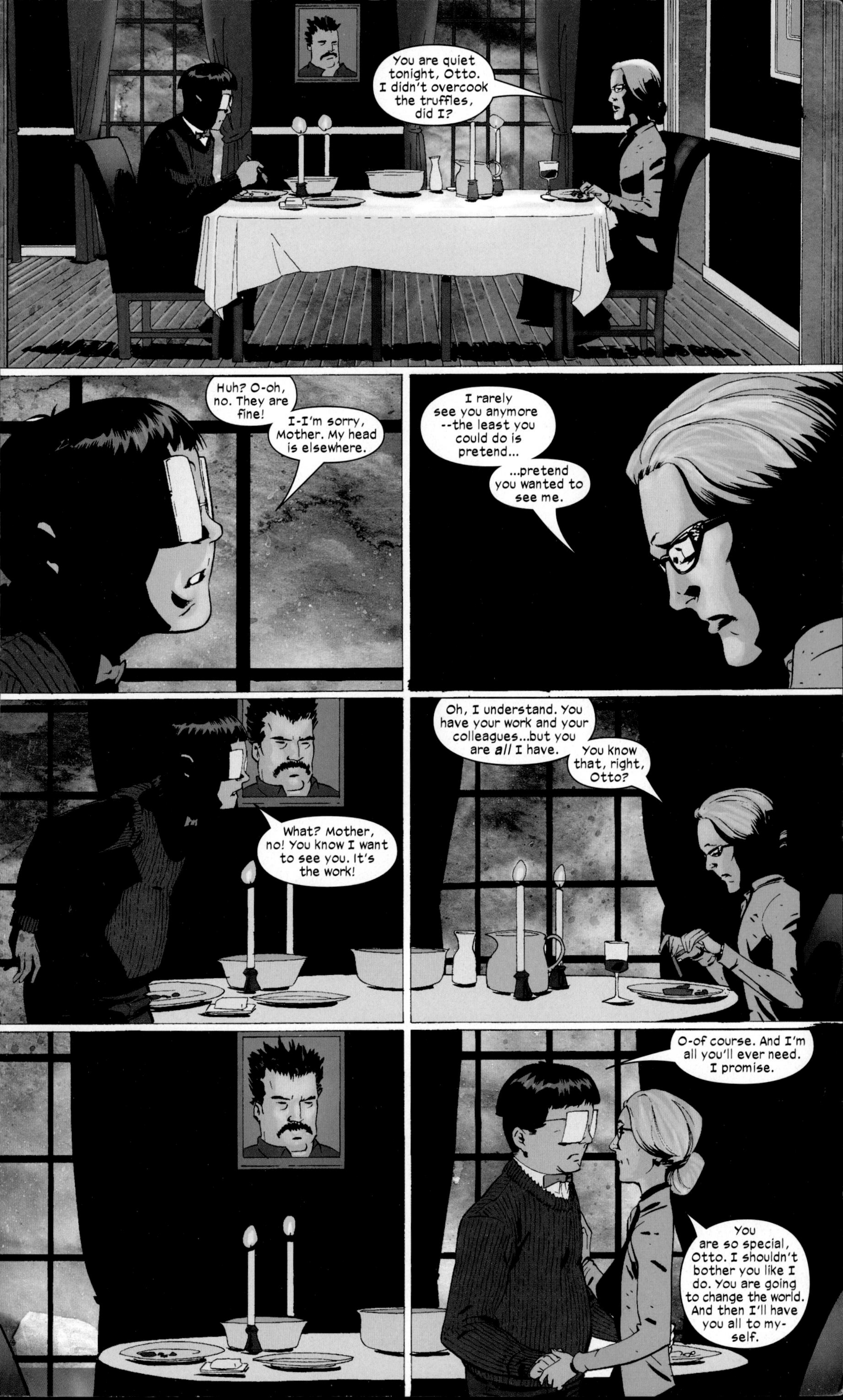
You are quiet tonight, Otto. I didn't overcook the truffles, did I?
Huh? O-oh, no. They are fine!
I-I'm sorry, Mother. My head is elsewhere.
I rarely see you anymore --the least you could do is pretend...
...pretend you wanted to see me.
What? Mother, no! You know I want to see you. It's the work!
Oh, I understand. You have your work and your colleagues...but you are *all* I have.
You know that, right, Otto?
O-of course. And I'm all you'll ever need. I promise.
You are so special, Otto. I shouldn't bother you like I do. You are going to change the world. And then I'll have you all to my-self.

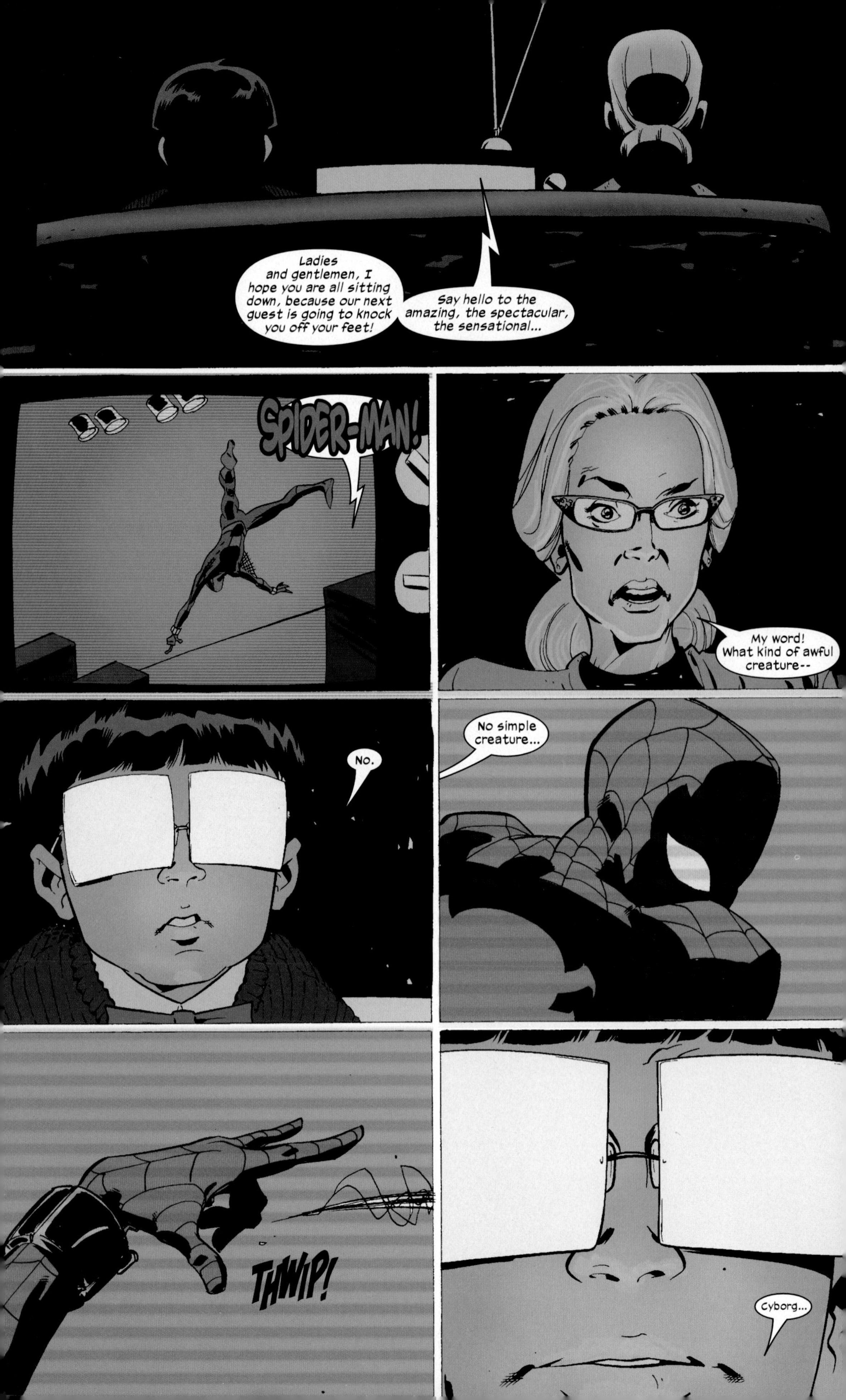
Ladies and gentlemen, I hope you are all sitting down, because our next guest is going to knock you off your feet!
Say hello to the amazing, the spectacular, the sensational...
SPIDER-MAN!
My word! What kind of awful creature--
No.
No simple creature...
THWIP!
Cyborg...

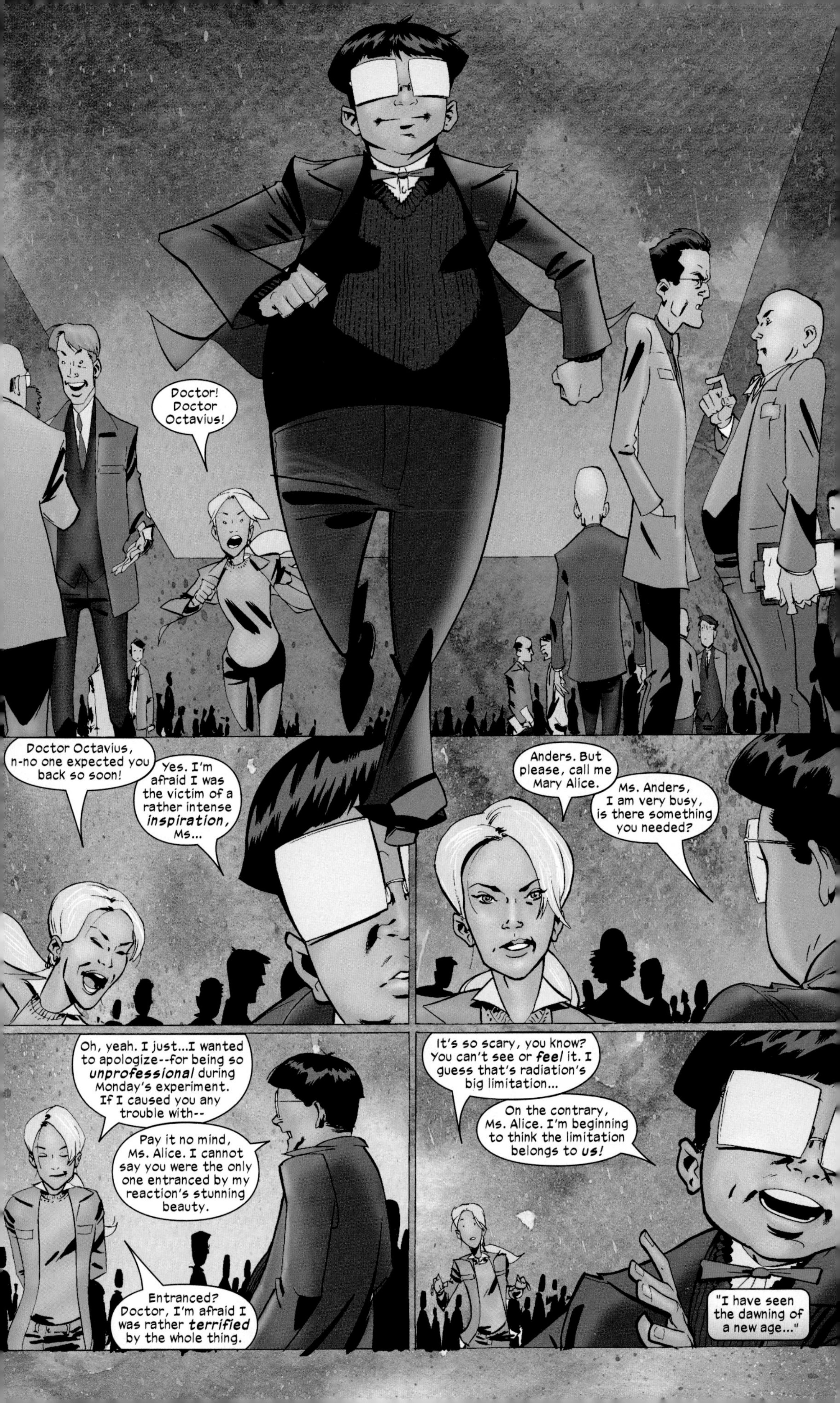
Doctor! Doctor Octavius!
Doctor Octavius, n-no one expected you back so soon!
Yes. I'm afraid I was the victim of a rather intense *inspiration*, Ms...
Anders. But please, call me Mary Alice.
Ms. Anders, I am very busy, is there something you needed?
Oh, yeah. I just...I wanted to apologize--for being so *unprofessional* during Monday's experiment. If I caused you any trouble with--
Pay it no mind, Ms. Alice. I cannot say you were the only one entranced by my reaction's stunning beauty.
Entranced? Doctor, I'm afraid I was rather ***terrified*** by the whole thing.
It's so scary, you know? You can't see or *feel* it. I guess that's radiation's big limitation...
On the contrary, Ms. Alice. I'm beginning to think the limitation belongs to *us!*
"I have seen the dawning of a new age..."

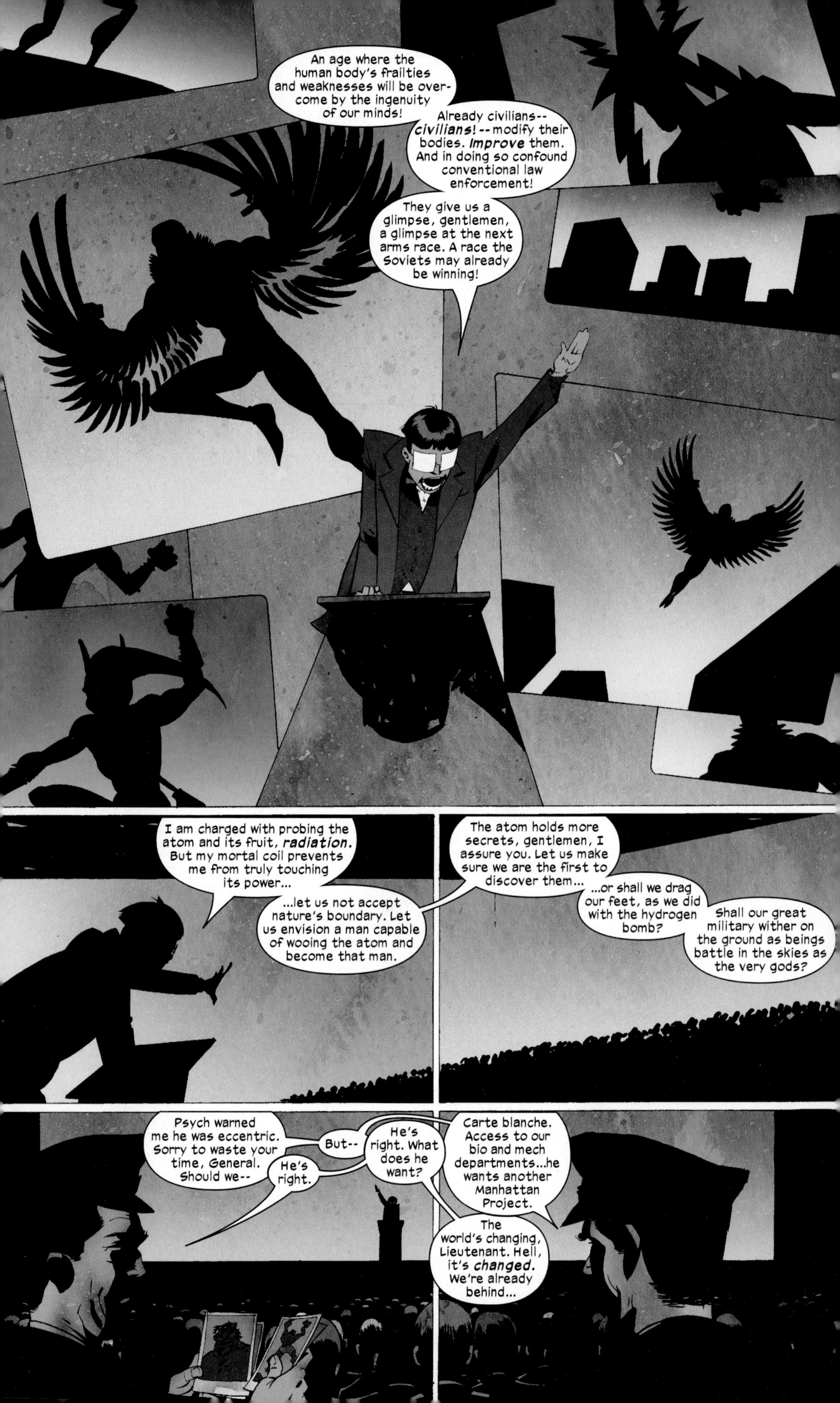
An age where the human body's frailties and weaknesses will be overcome by the ingenuity of our minds!
Already civilians-- *civilians!* --modify their bodies. *Improve* them. And in doing so confound conventional law enforcement!
They give us a glimpse, gentlemen, a glimpse at the next arms race. A race the Soviets may already be winning!
I am charged with probing the atom and its fruit, *radiation.* But my mortal coil prevents me from truly touching its power...
...let us not accept nature's boundary. Let us envision a man capable of wooing the atom and become that man.
The atom holds more secrets, gentlemen, I assure you. Let us make sure we are the first to discover them...
...or shall we drag our feet, as we did with the hydrogen bomb?
Shall our great military wither on the ground as beings battle in the skies as the very gods?
Psych warned me he was eccentric. Sorry to waste your time, General. Should we--
But--
He's right.
He's right. What does he want?
Carte blanche. Access to our bio and mech departments...he wants another Manhattan Project.
The world's changing, Lieutenant. Hell, it's *changed.* We're already behind...

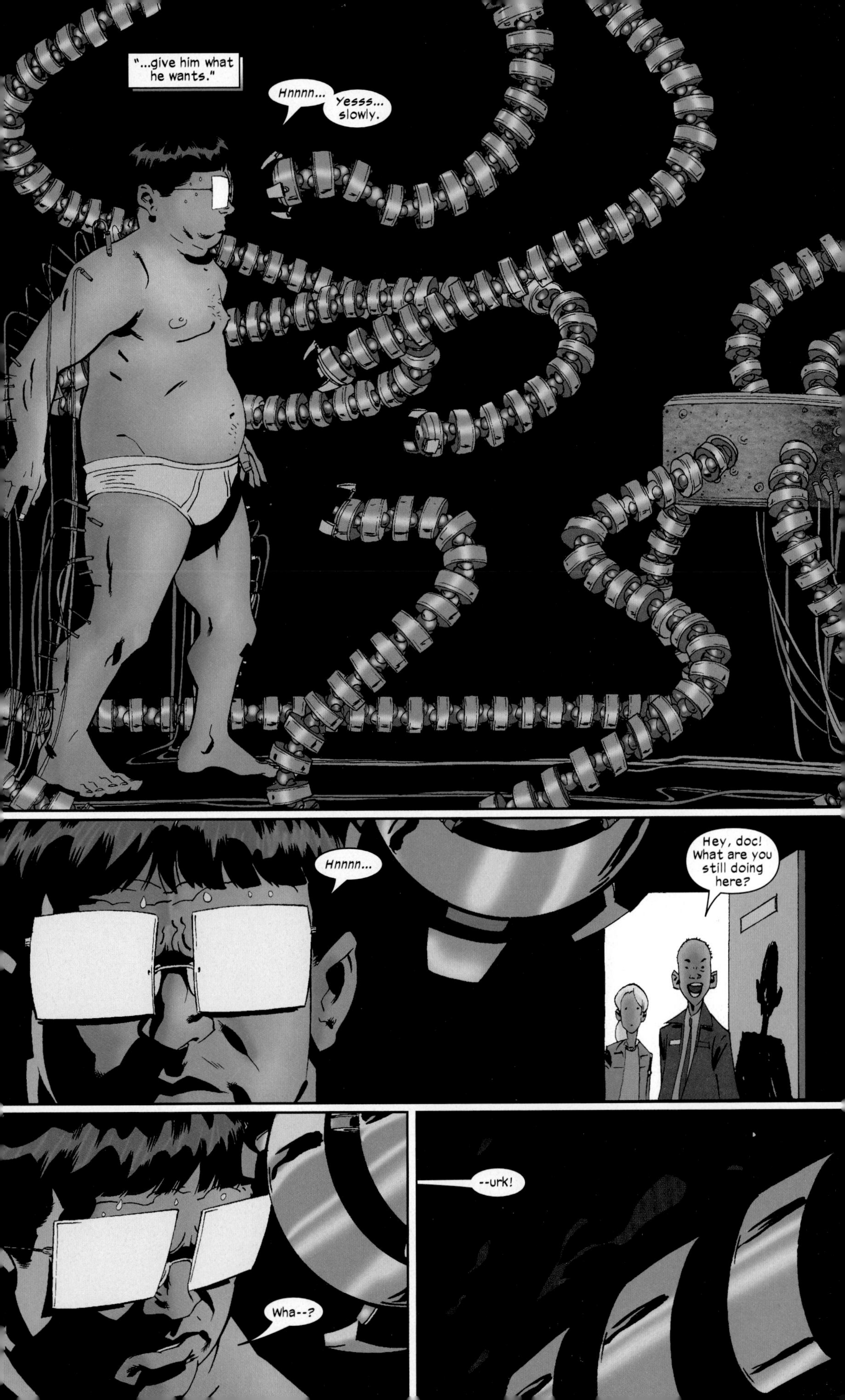
"...give him what he wants."
Hnnnn...
Yesss... slowly.
Hnnnn...
Hey, doc! What are you still doing here?
Wha--?
--urk!

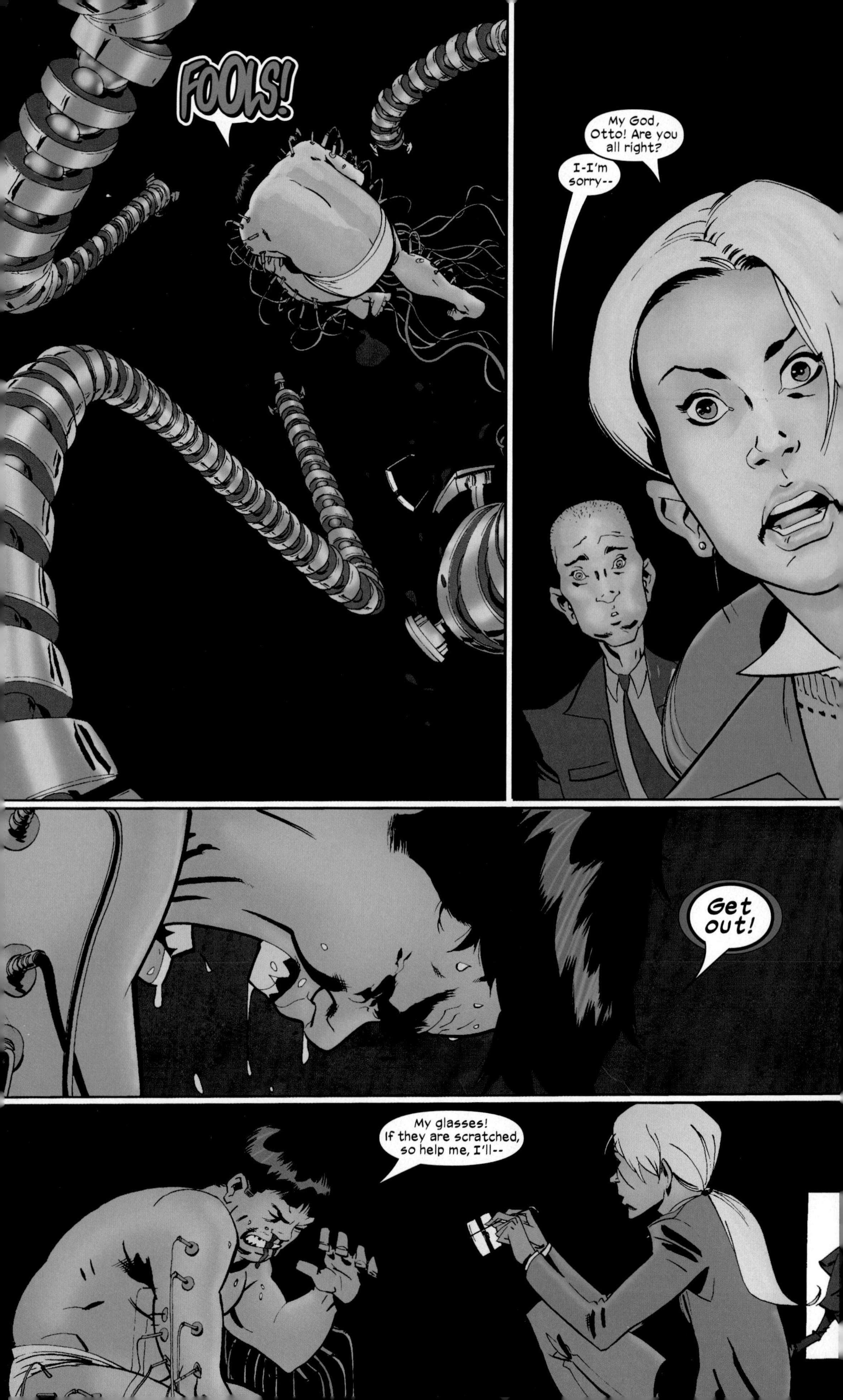
FOOLS!
My God, Otto! Are you all right?
I-I'm sorry--
Get out!
My glasses! If they are scratched, so help me, I'll--

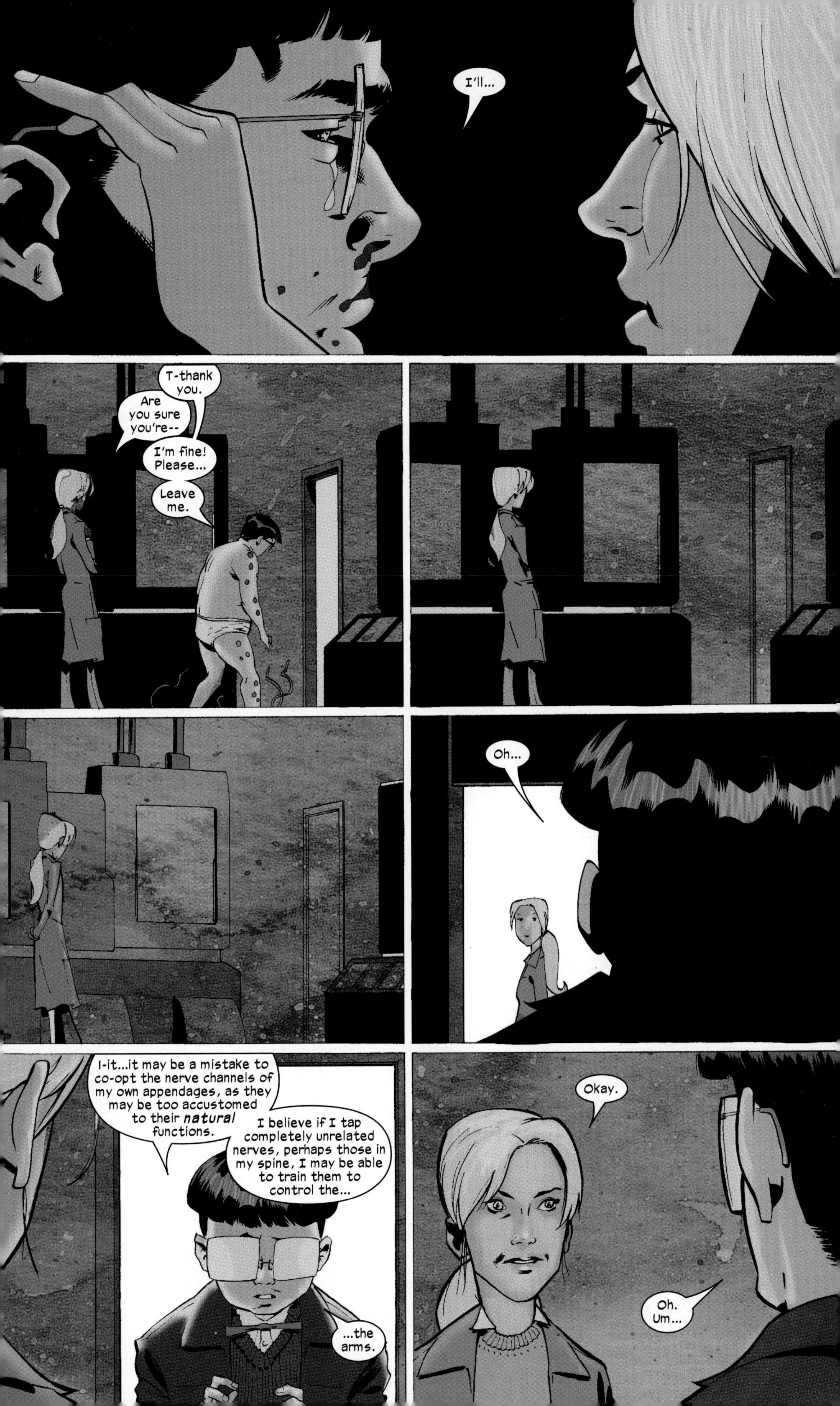

I'll...
T-thank you.
Are you sure you're--
I'm fine! Please...
Leave me.
Oh...
I-it...it may be a mistake to co-opt the nerve channels of my own appendages, as they may be too accustomed to their *natural* functions.
I believe if I tap completely unrelated nerves, perhaps those in my spine, I may be able to train them to control the...
...the arms.
Okay.
Oh. Um...

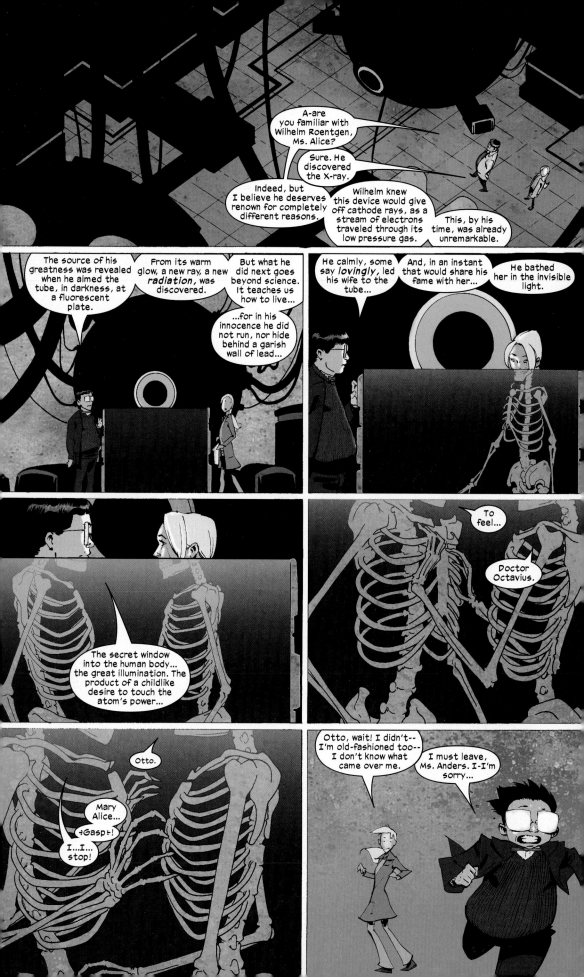

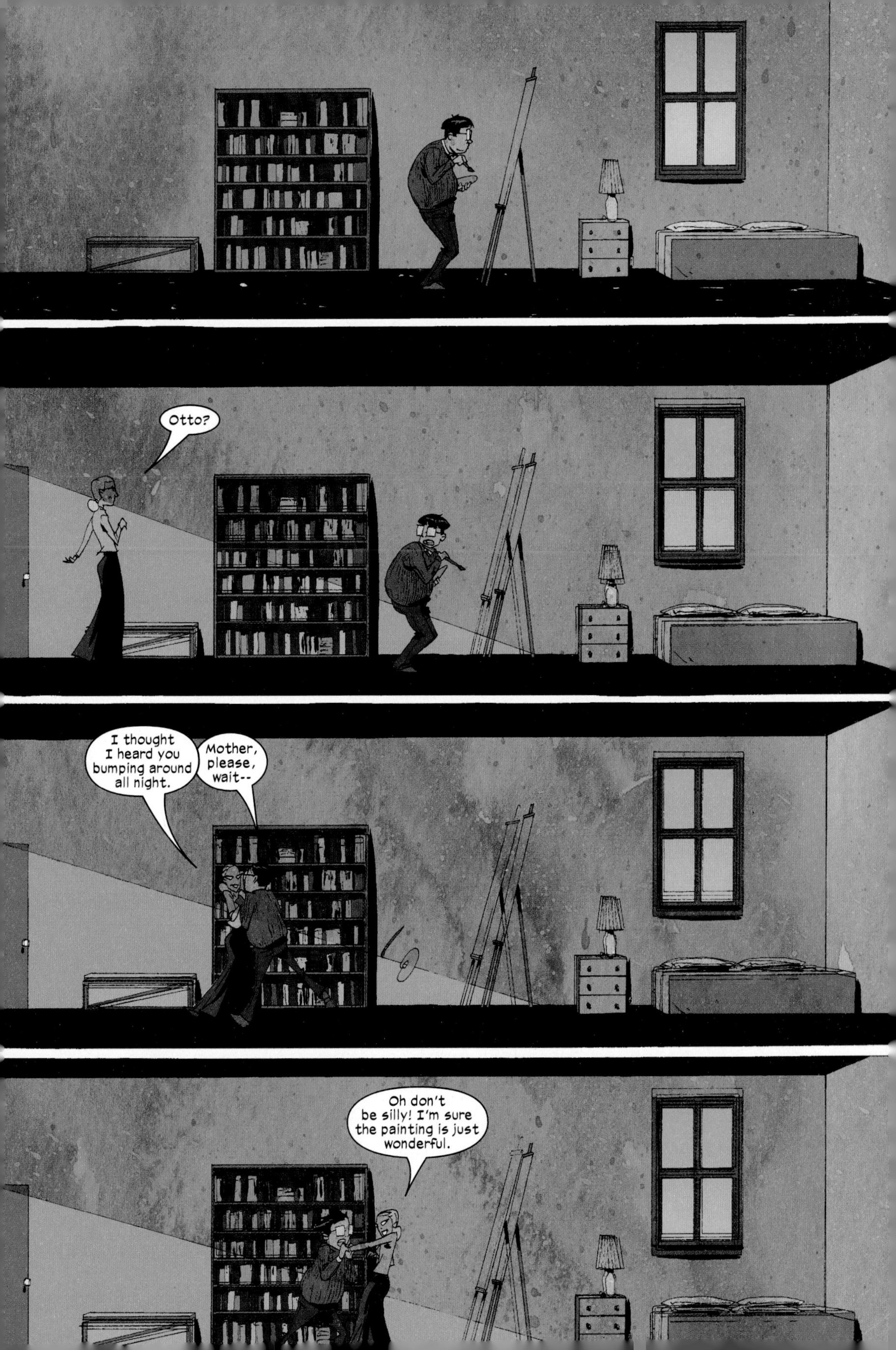
Otto?
I thought I heard you bumping around all night.
Mother, please, wait--
Oh don't be silly! I'm sure the painting is just wonderful.

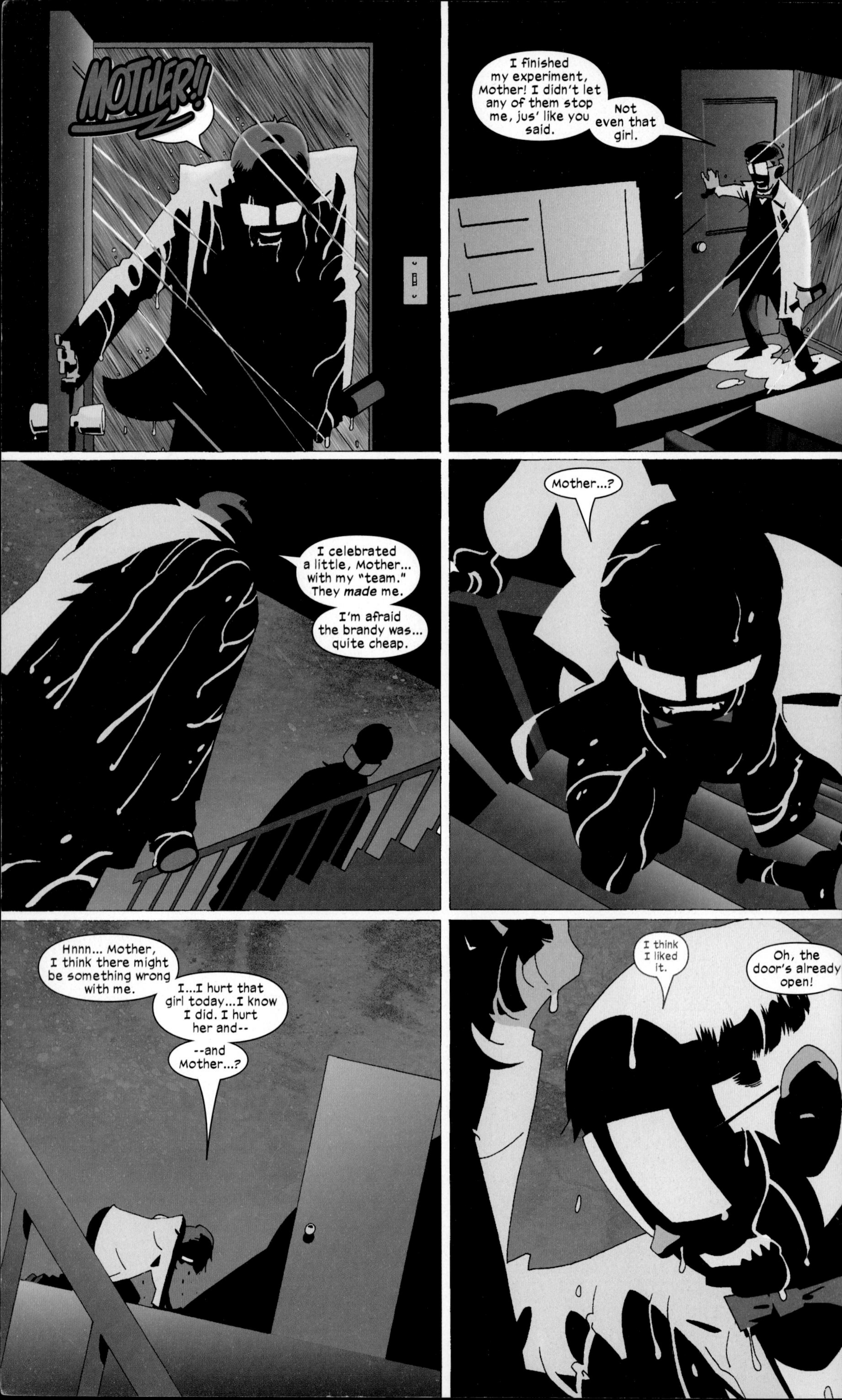
MOTHER!!
I finished my experiment, Mother! I didn't let any of them stop me, jus' like you said.
Not even that girl.
I celebrated a little, Mother... with my "team." They *made* me.
I'm afraid the brandy was... quite cheap.
Mother...?
Hnnn... Mother, I think there might be something wrong with me.
I...I hurt that girl today...I know I did. I hurt her and--
--and Mother...?
I think I liked it.
Oh, the door's already open!

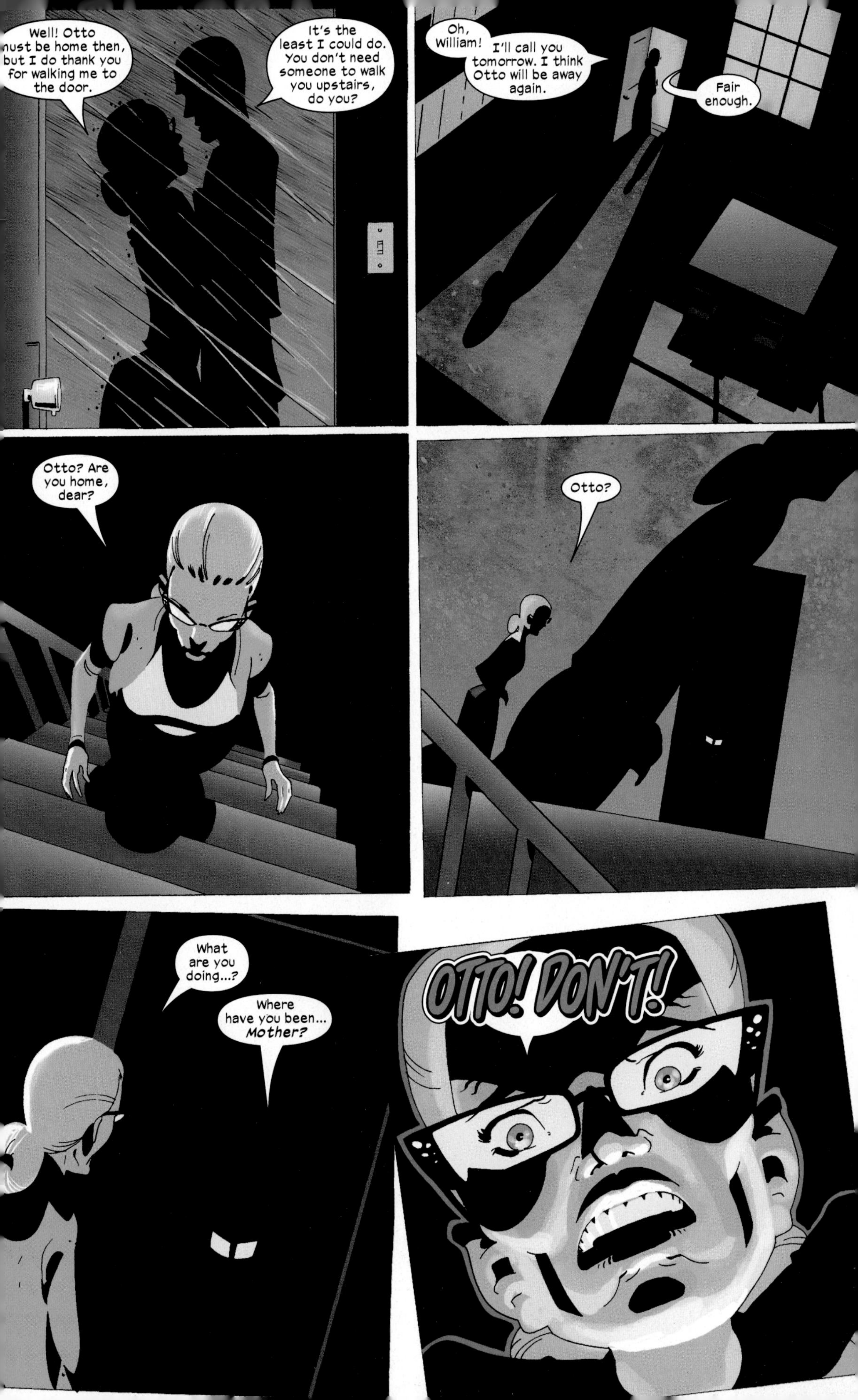

Well! Otto nust be home then, but I do thank you for walking me to the door.
It's the least I could do. You don't need someone to walk you upstairs, do you?
Oh, William!
I'll call you tomorrow. I think Otto will be away again.
Fair enough.
Otto? Are you home, dear?
Otto?
What are you doing...?
Where have you been... *Mother?*
OTTO! DON'T!

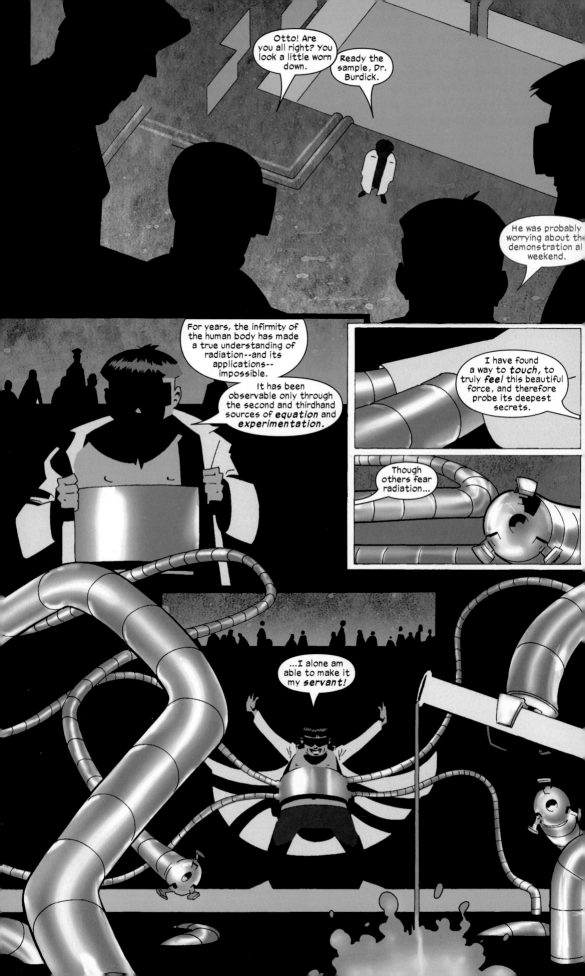

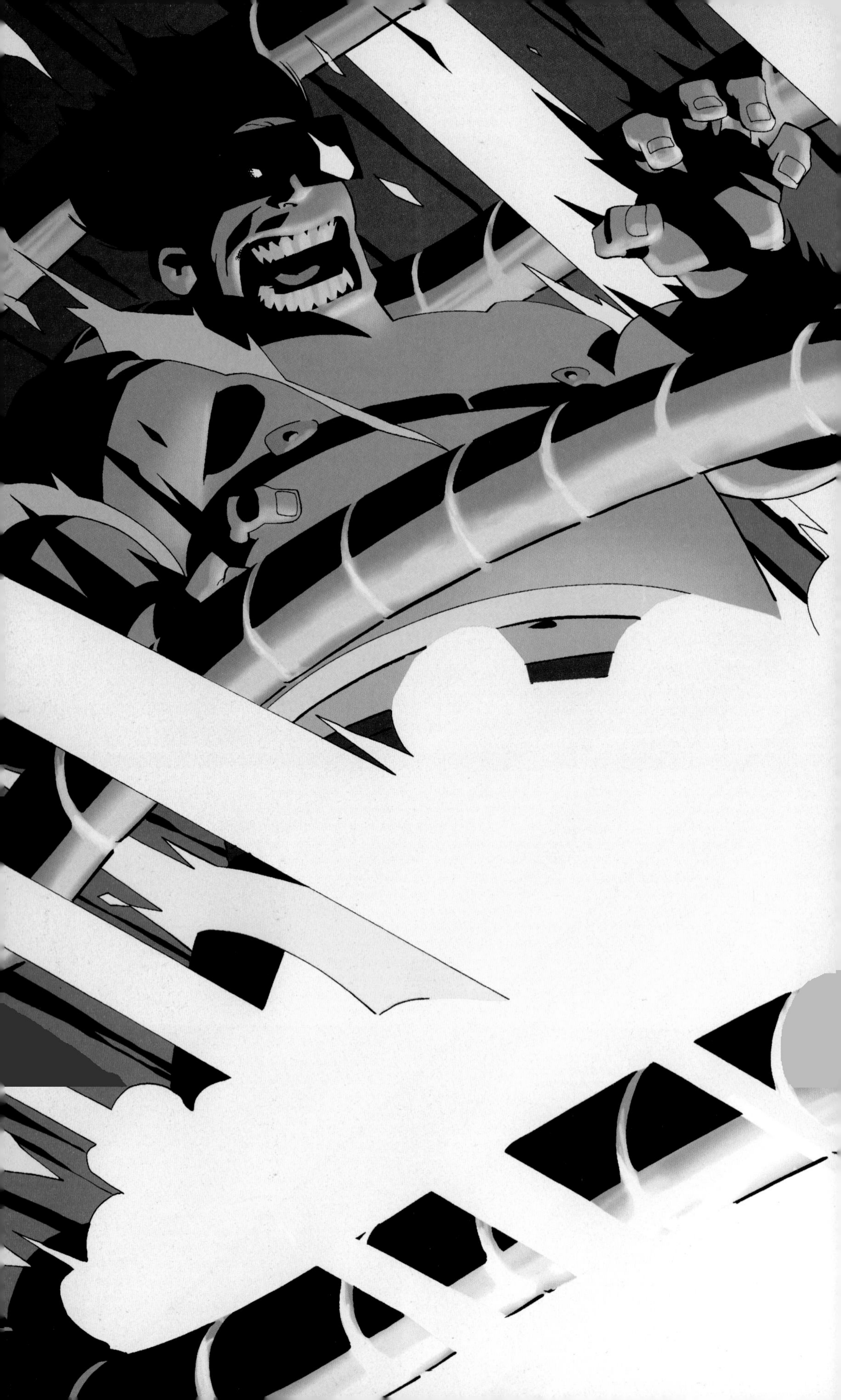

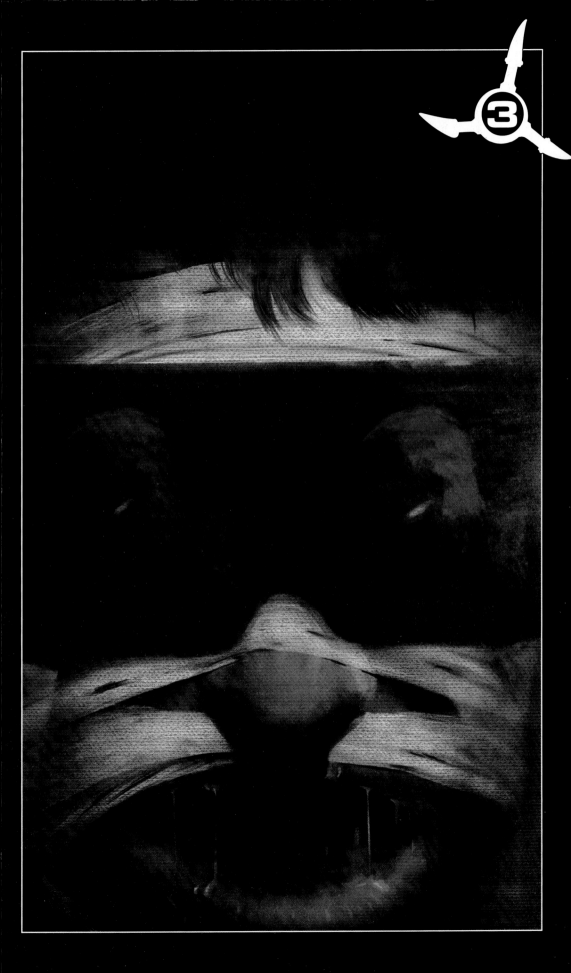

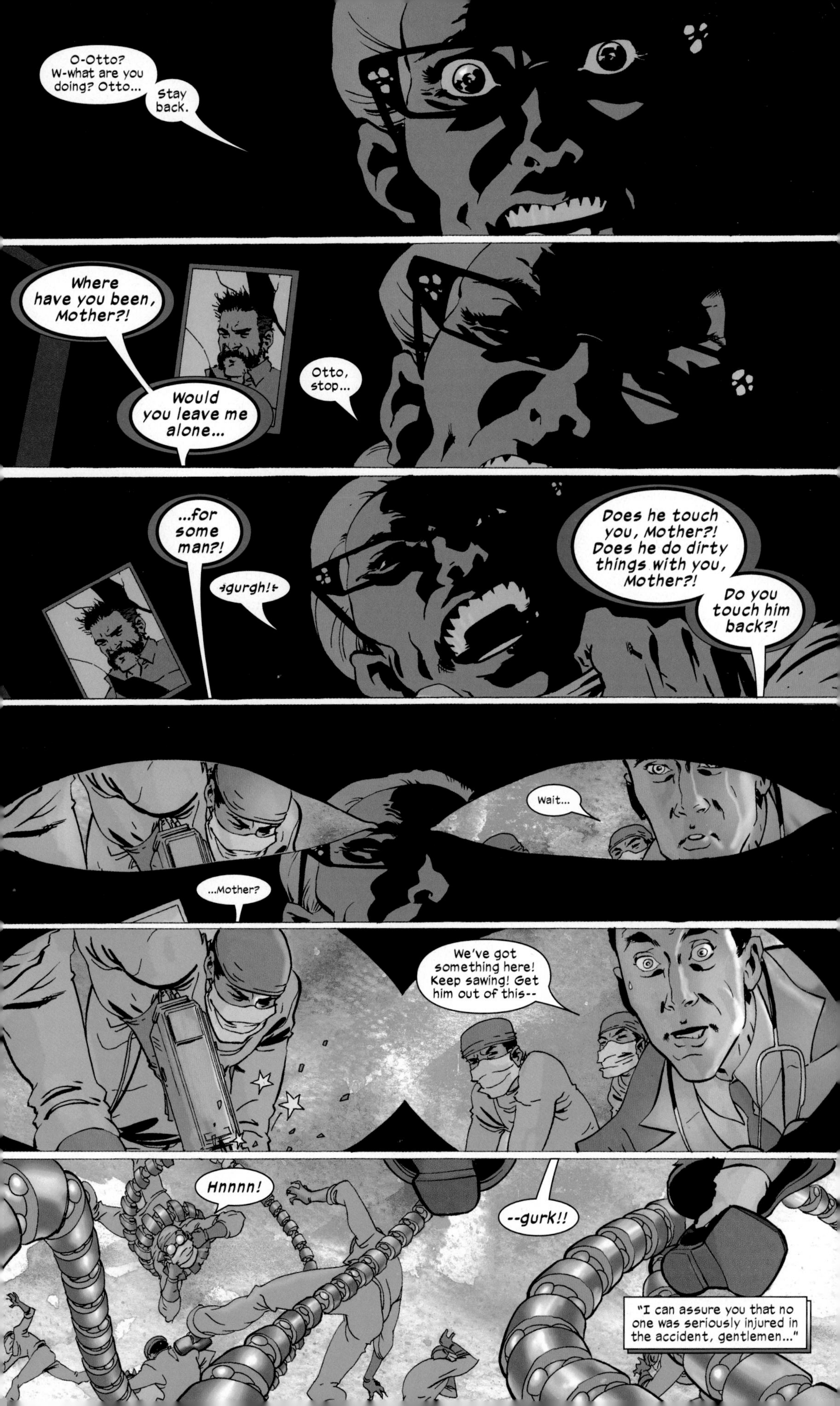
O-Otto? W-what are you doing? Otto...
Stay back.
Where have you been, Mother?!
Would you leave me alone...
Otto, stop...
...for some man?!
-gurgh!-
Does he touch you, Mother?! Does he do dirty things with you, Mother?!
Do you touch him back?!
Wait...
...Mother?
We've got something here! Keep sawing! Get him out of this--
Hnnnn!
--gurk!!
"I can assure you that no one was seriously injured in the accident, gentlemen..."

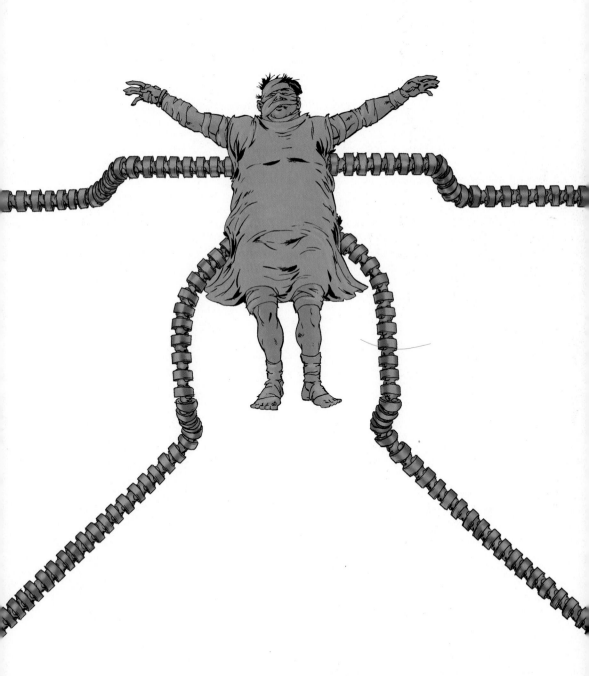

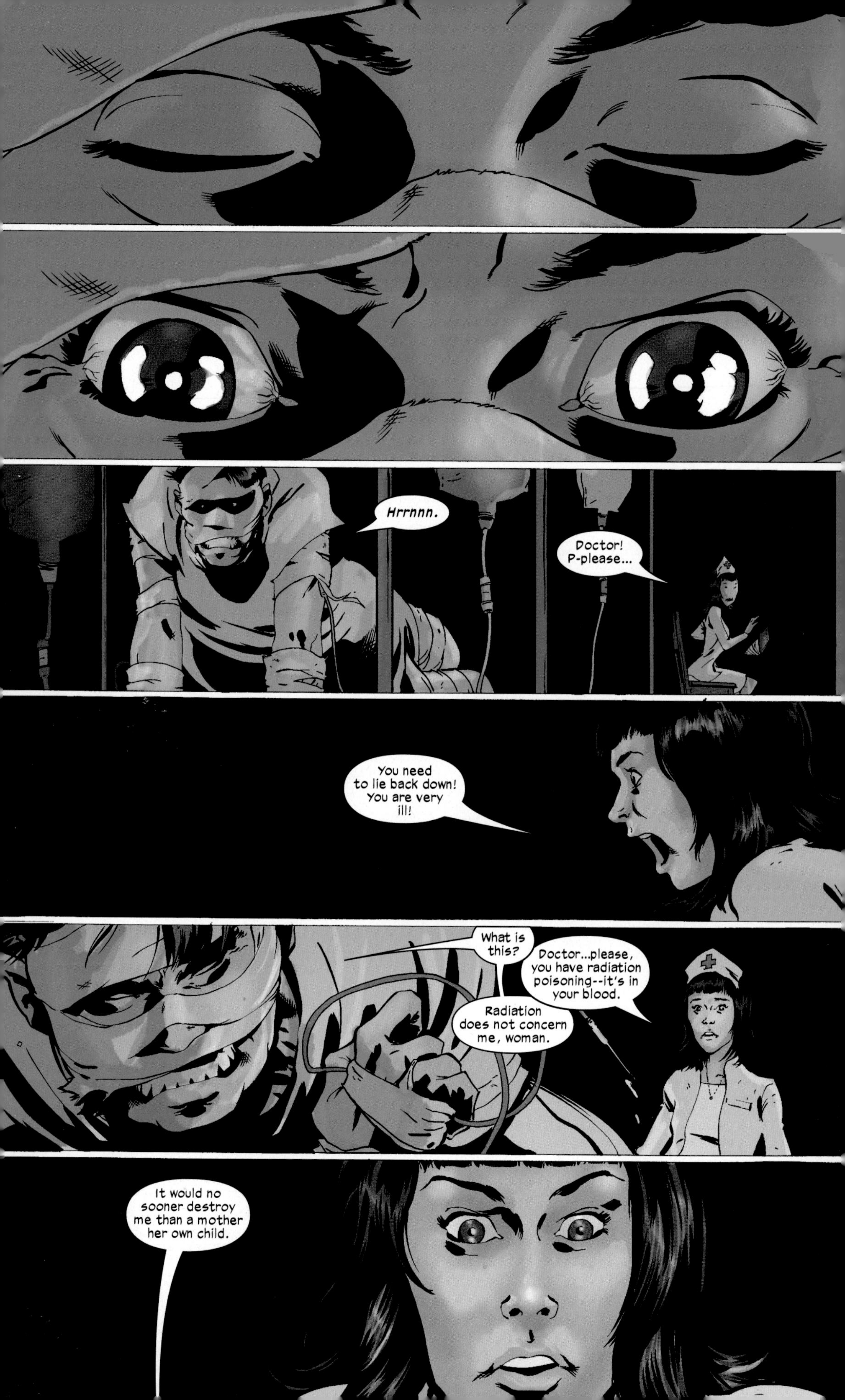
Hrrnnn.
Doctor! P-please...
You need to lie back down! You are very ill!
What is this?
Doctor...please, you have radiation poisoning--it's in your blood.
Radiation does not concern me, woman.
It would no sooner destroy me than a mother her own child.

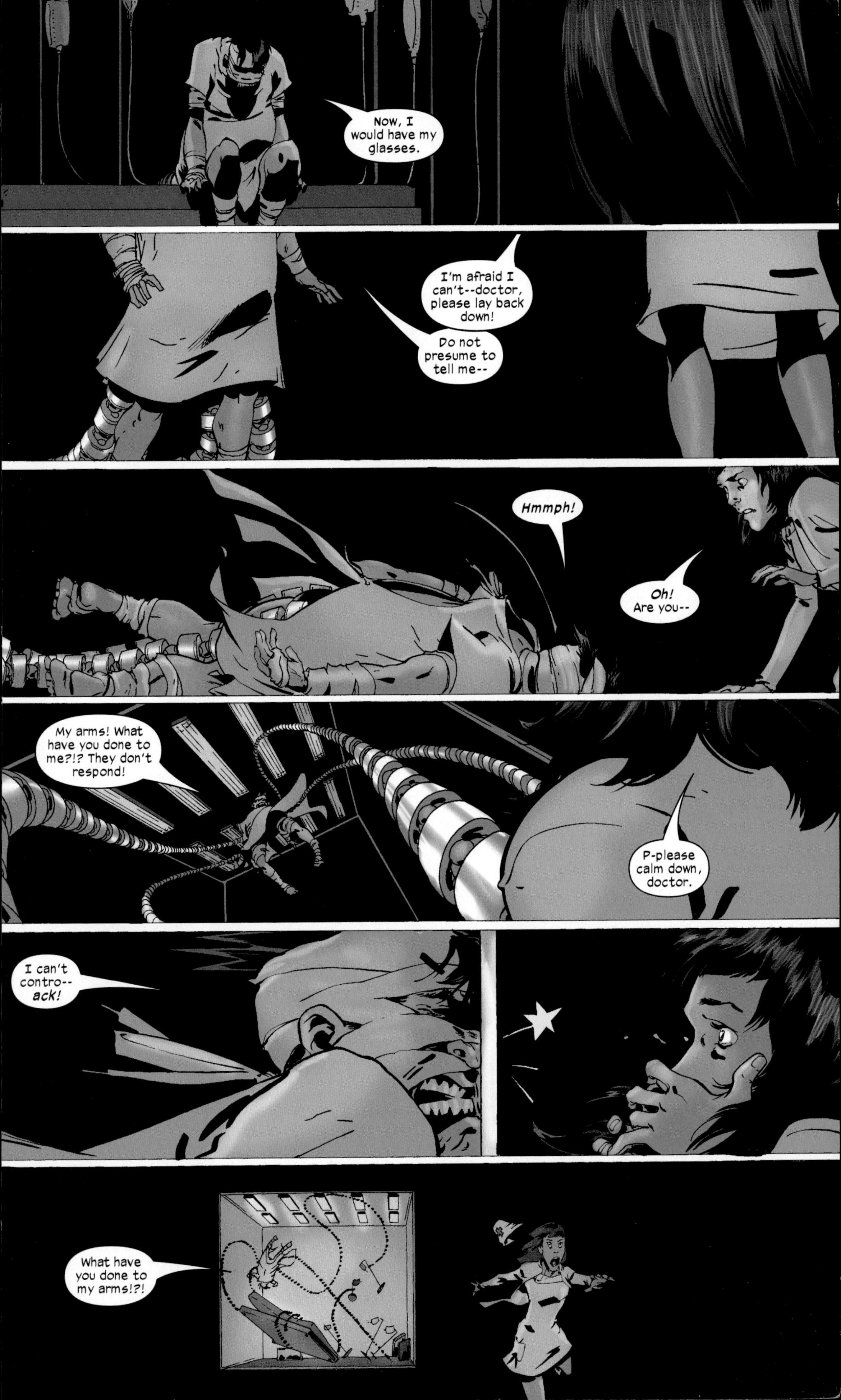
Now, I would have my glasses.
I'm afraid I can't--doctor, please lay back down!
Do not presume to tell me--
Hmmph!
Oh! Are you--
My arms! What have you done to me?!? They don't respond!
P-please calm down, doctor.
I can't contro-- ack!
What have you done to my arms!?!

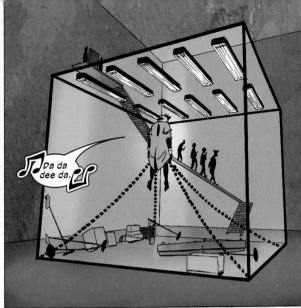

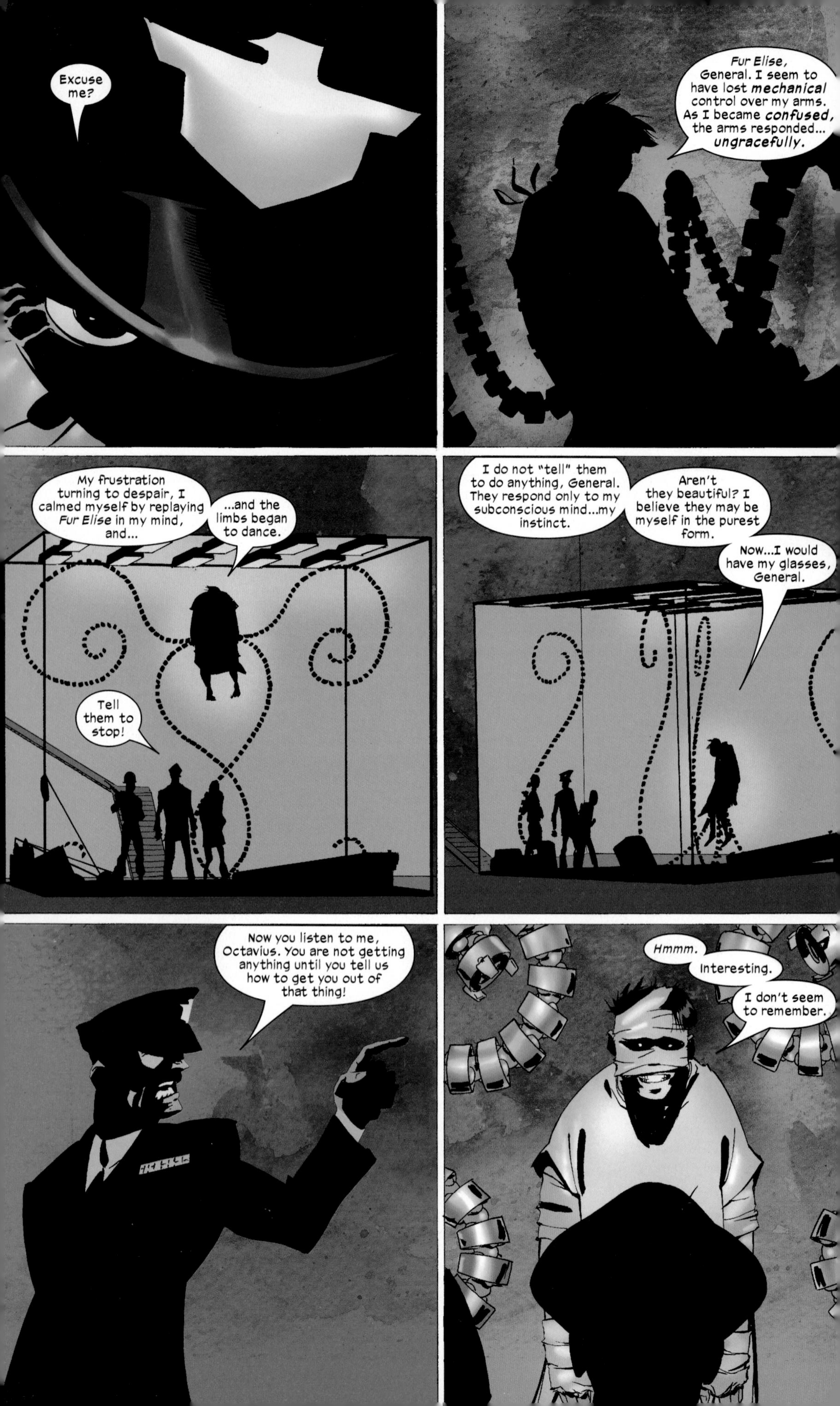
Excuse me?
Fur Elise, General. I seem to have lost mechanical control over my arms. As I became confused, the arms responded... ungracefully.
My frustration turning to despair, I calmed myself by replaying Fur Elise in my mind, and...
...and the limbs began to dance.
Tell them to stop!
I do not "tell" them to do anything, General. They respond only to my subconscious mind...my instinct.
Aren't they beautiful? I believe they may be myself in the purest form.
Now...I would have my glasses, General.
Now you listen to me, Octavius. You are not getting anything until you tell us how to get you out of that thing!
Hmmm.
Interesting.
I don't seem to remember.

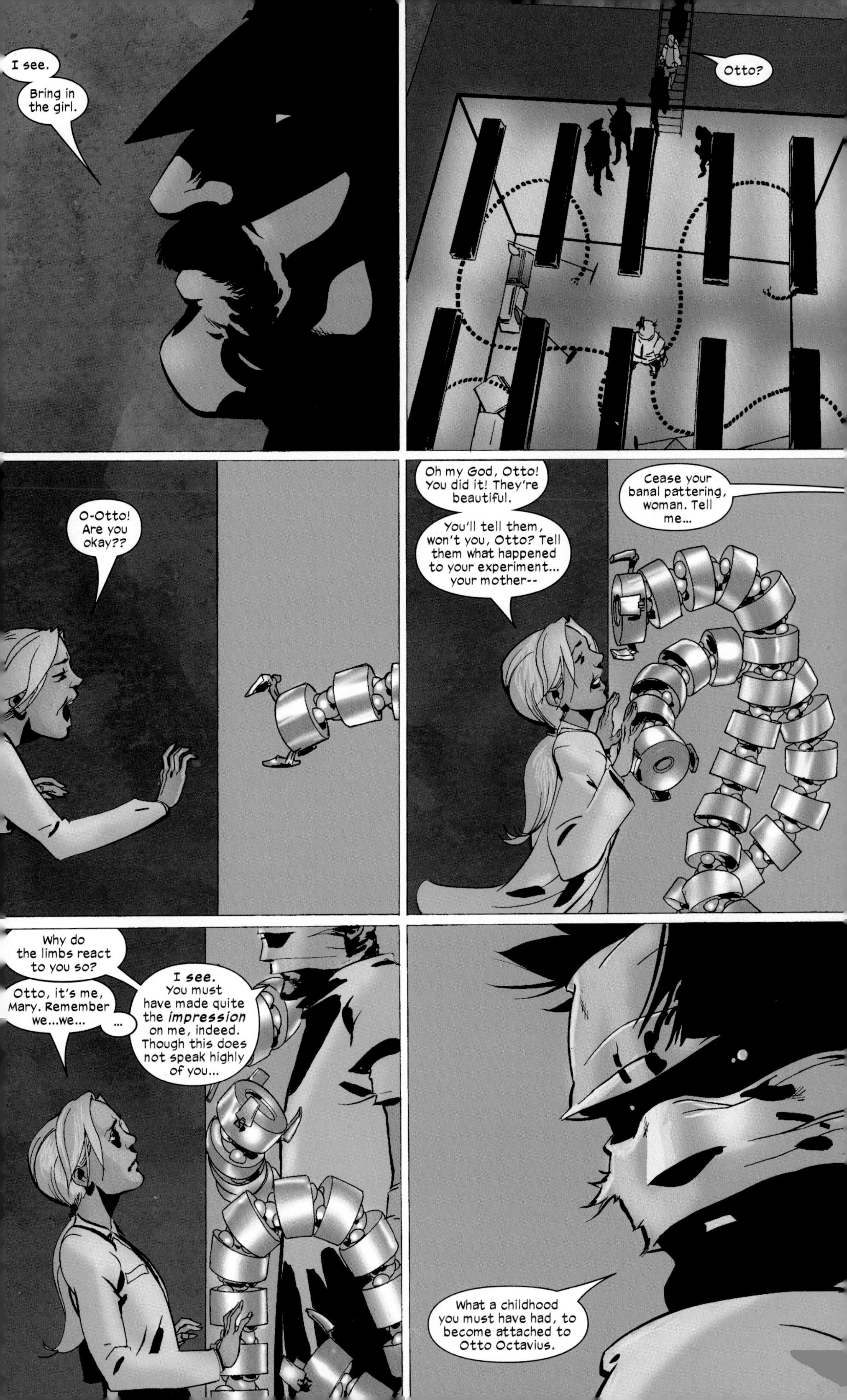
I see.
Bring in the girl.
Otto?
O-Otto! Are you okay??
Oh my God, Otto! You did it! They're beautiful.
You'll tell them, won't you, Otto? Tell them what happened to your experiment... your mother--
Cease your banal pattering, woman. Tell me...
Why do the limbs react to you so?
Otto, it's me, Mary. Remember we...we...
...
I *see.* You must have made quite the *impression* on me, indeed. Though this does not speak highly of you...
What a childhood you must have had, to become attached to Otto Octavius.

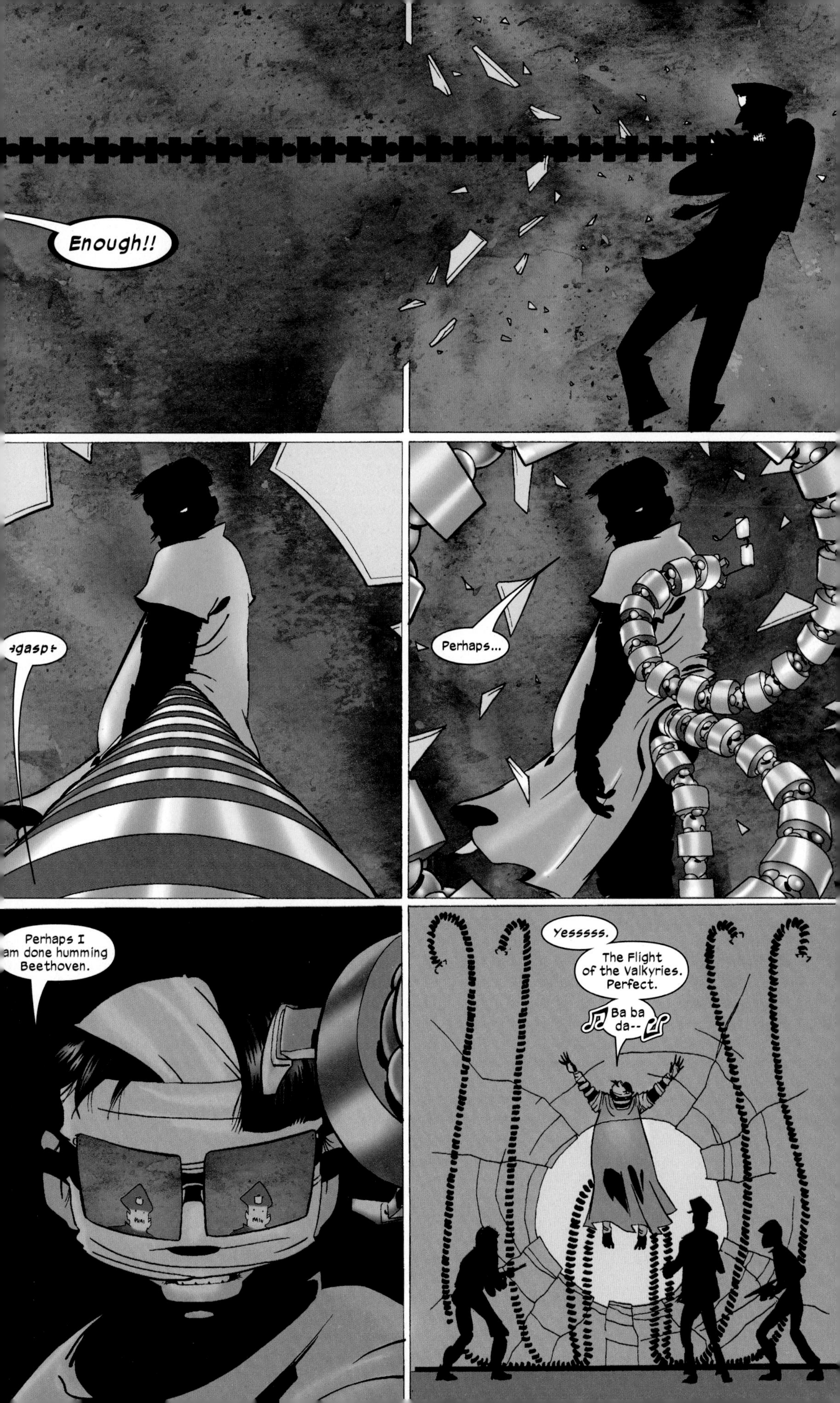
Enough!!
+gasp+
Perhaps...
Perhaps I am done humming Beethoven.
Yesssss.
The Flight of the Valkyries. Perfect.
Ba ba da--

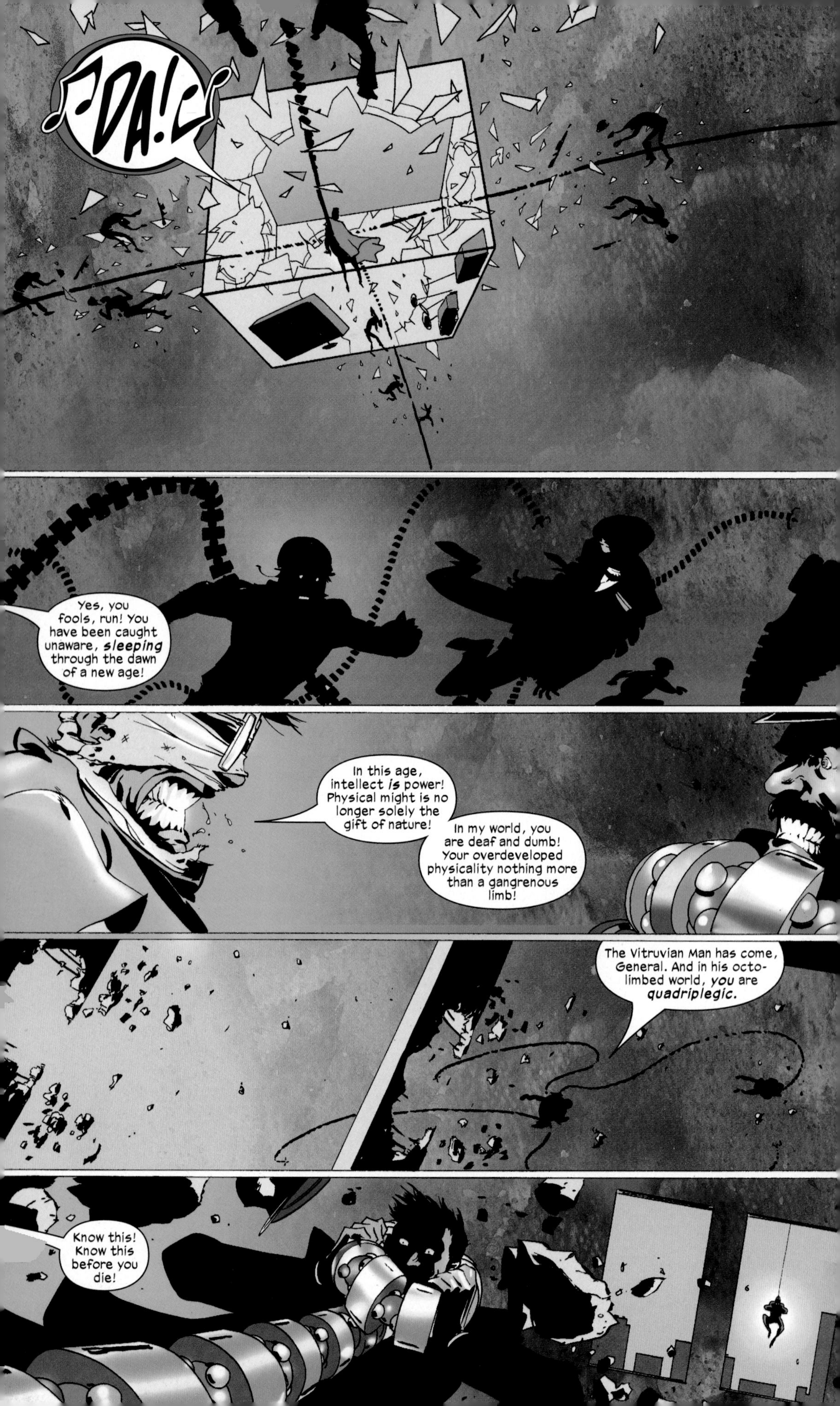
DA!
Yes, you fools, run! You have been caught unaware, *sleeping* through the dawn of a new age!
In this age, intellect *is* power! Physical might is no longer solely the gift of nature!
In my world, you are deaf and dumb! Your overdeveloped physicality nothing more than a gangrenous limb!
The Vitruvian Man has come, General. And in his octo-limbed world, *you* are *quadriplegic.*
Know this! Know this before you die!

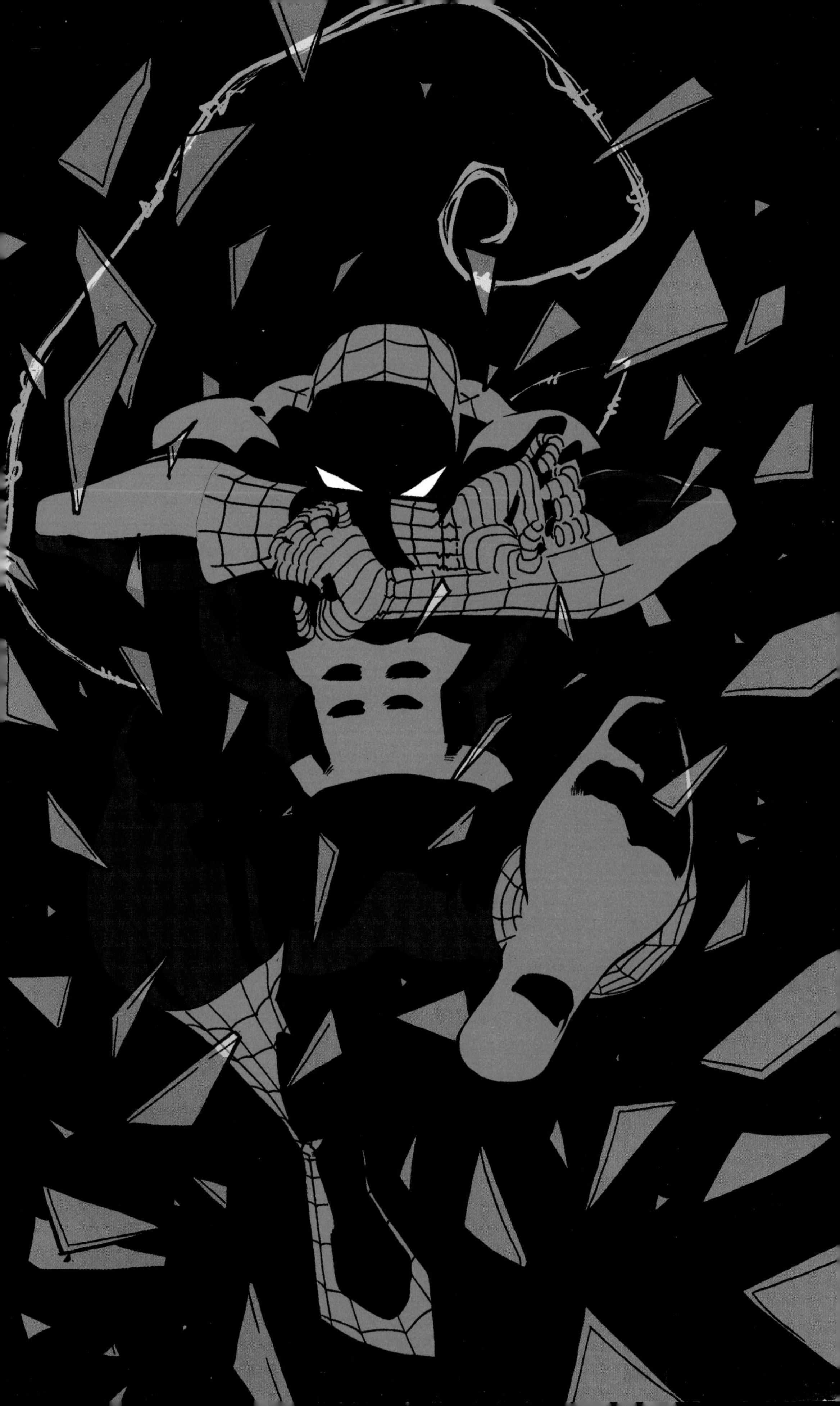

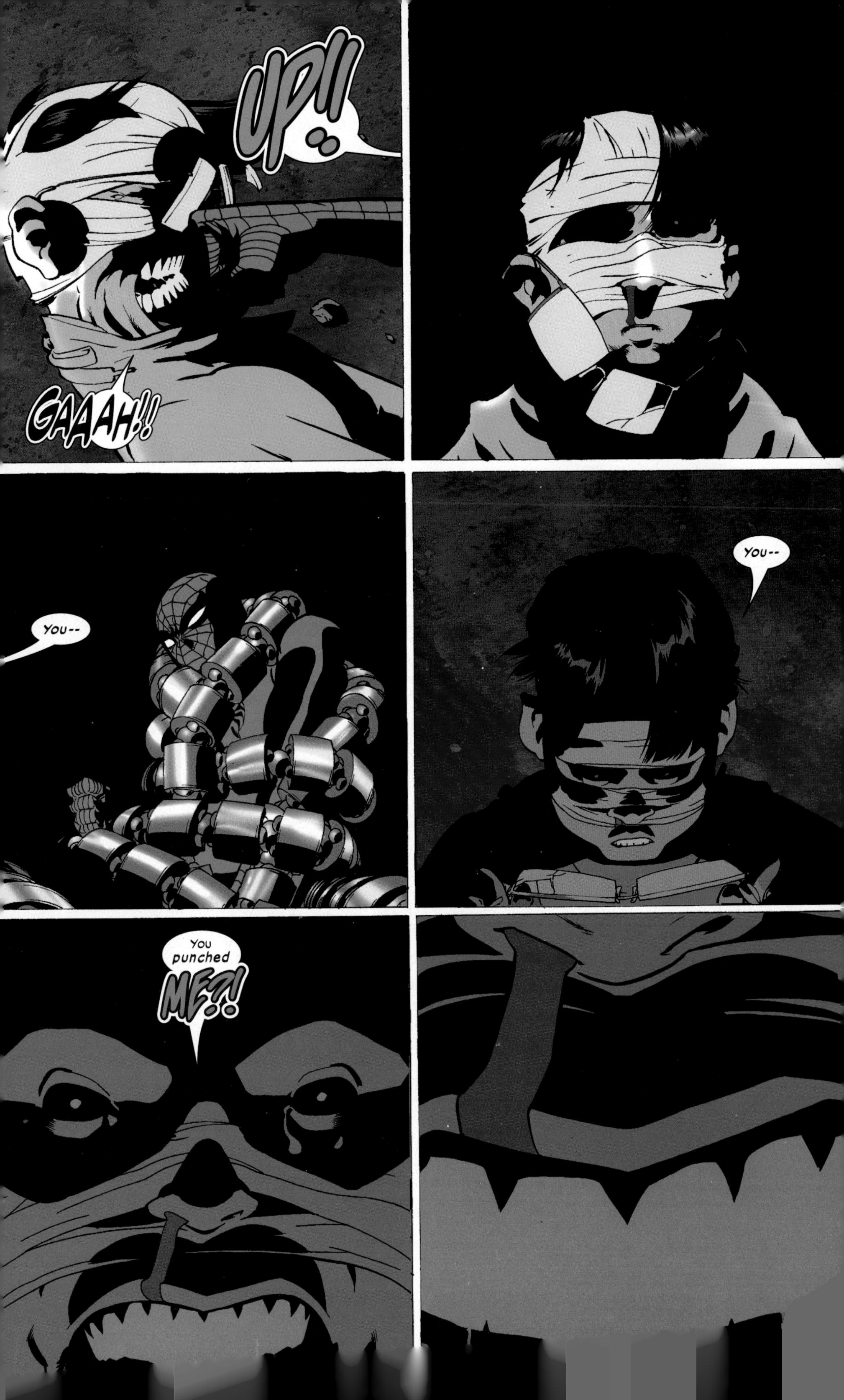
UP!!
GAAAH!!
You--
You--
You
punched
ME?!

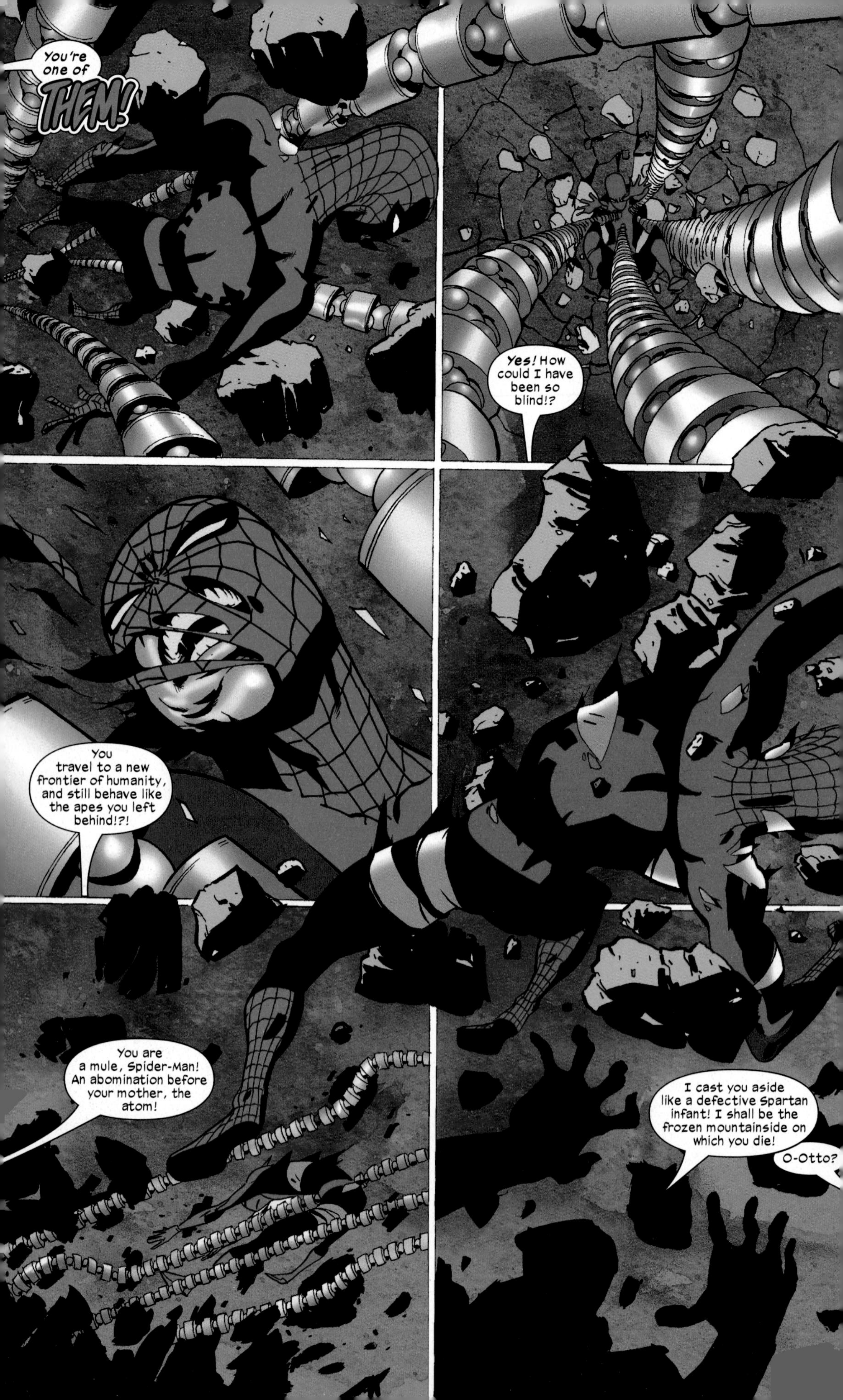
You're one of
THEM!
Yes! How could I have been so blind!?
You travel to a new frontier of humanity, and still behave like the apes you left behind!?!
You are a mule, Spider-Man! An abomination before your mother, the atom!
I cast you aside like a defective Spartan infant! I shall be the frozen mountainside on which you die!
O-Otto?

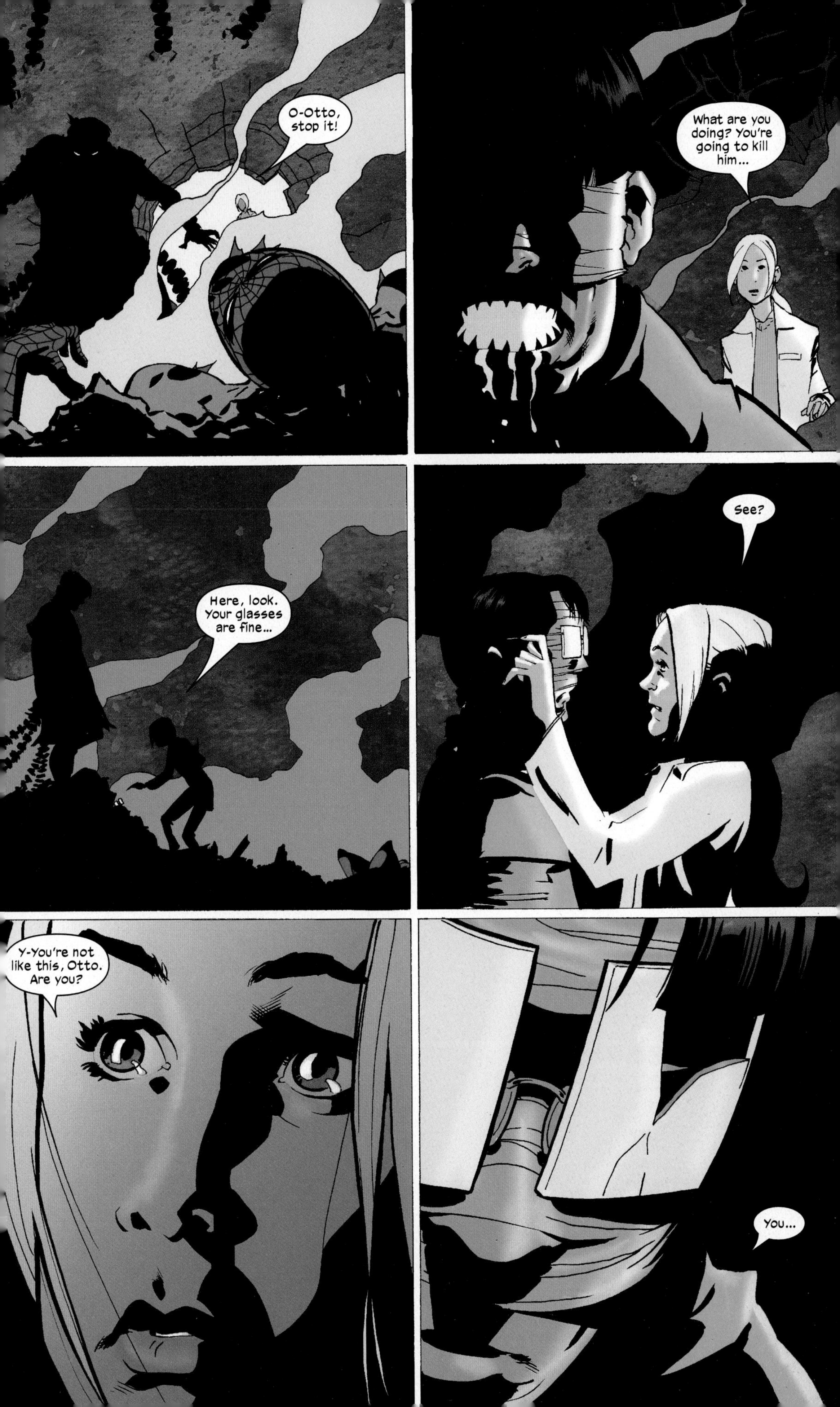
O-Otto, stop it!
What are you doing? You're going to kill him...
Here, look. Your glasses are fine...
See?
Y-You're not like this, Otto. Are you?
You...

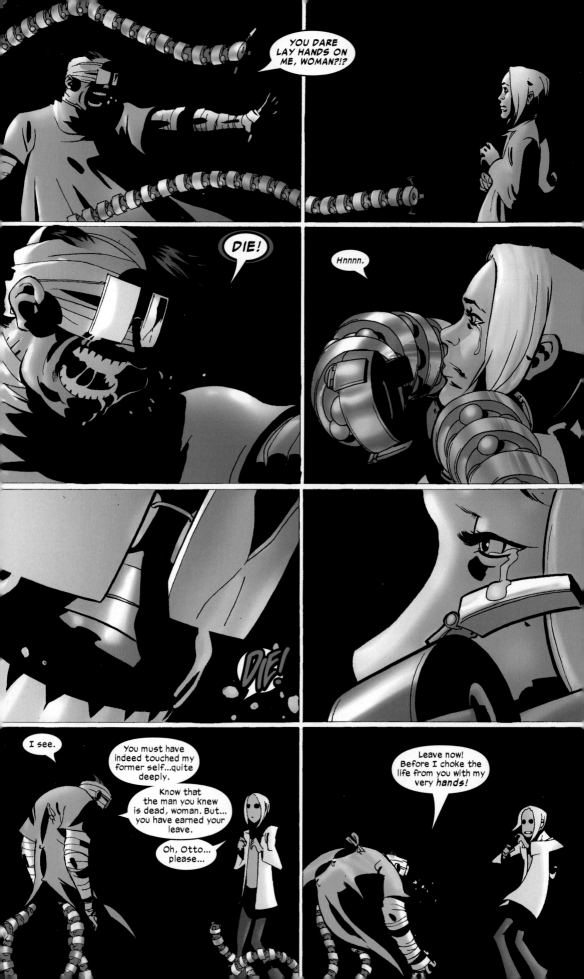

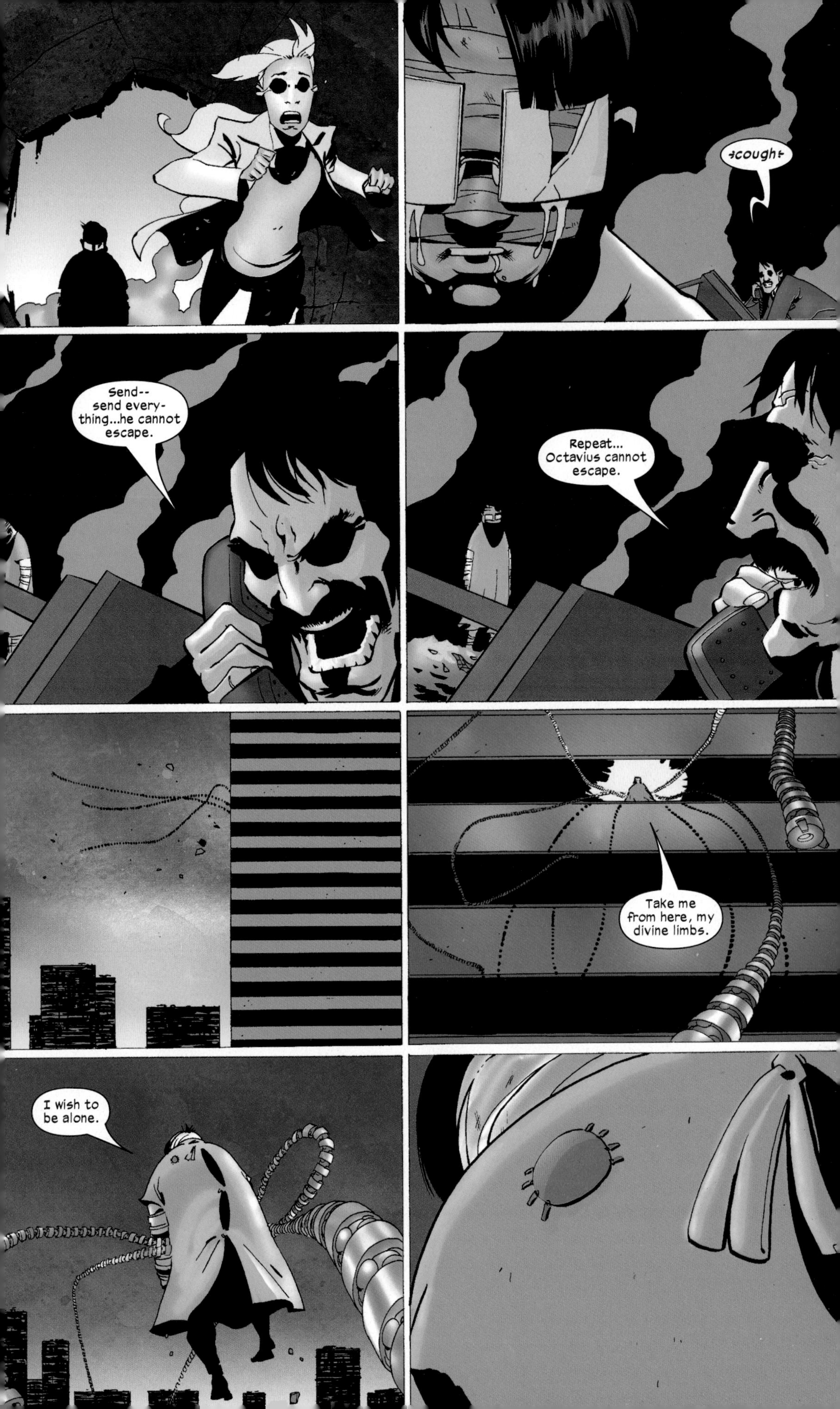

cough
Send--
send every-
thing...he cannot
escape.
Repeat...
Octavius cannot
escape.
Take me
from here, my
divine limbs.
I wish to
be alone.

4

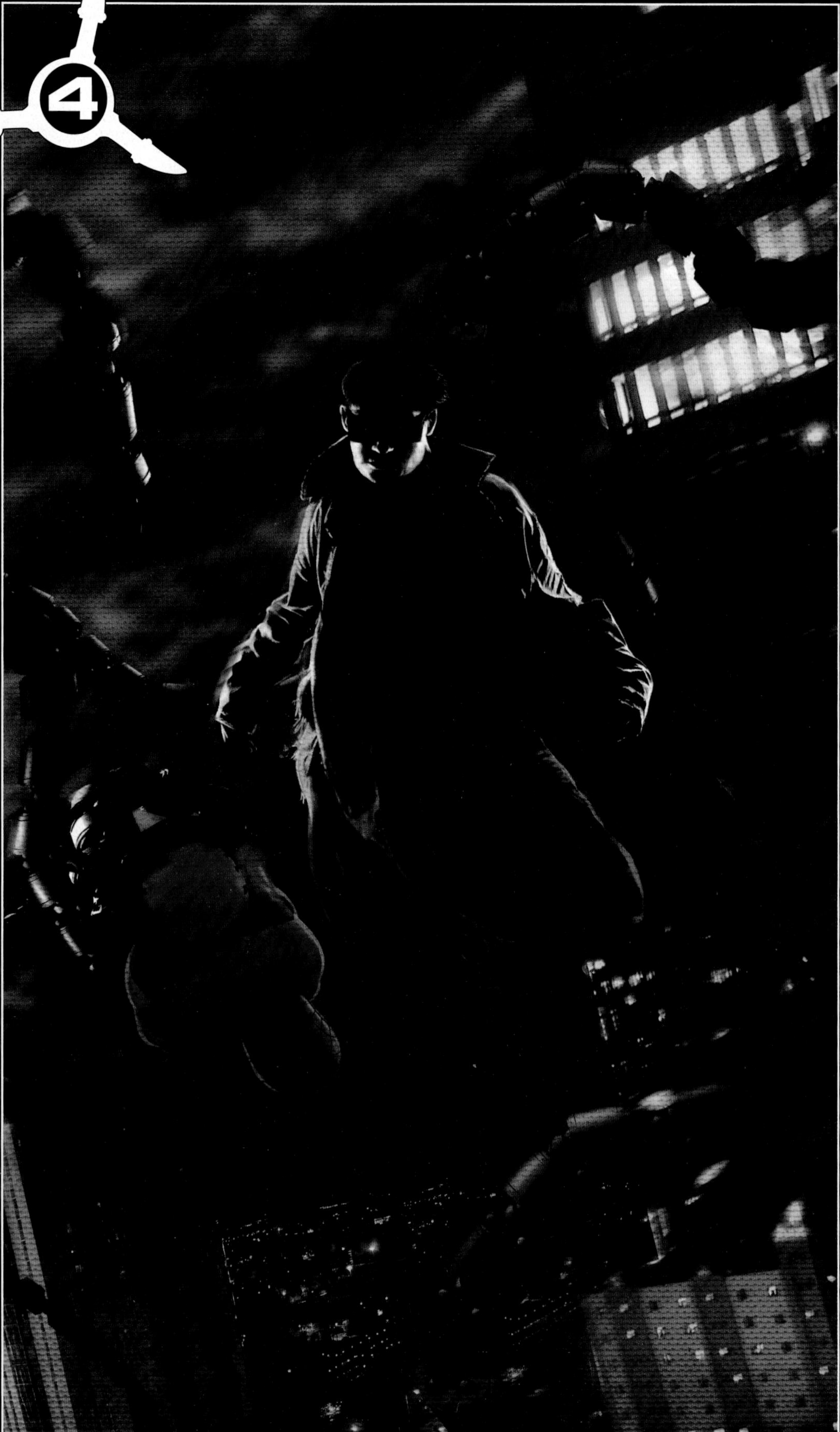

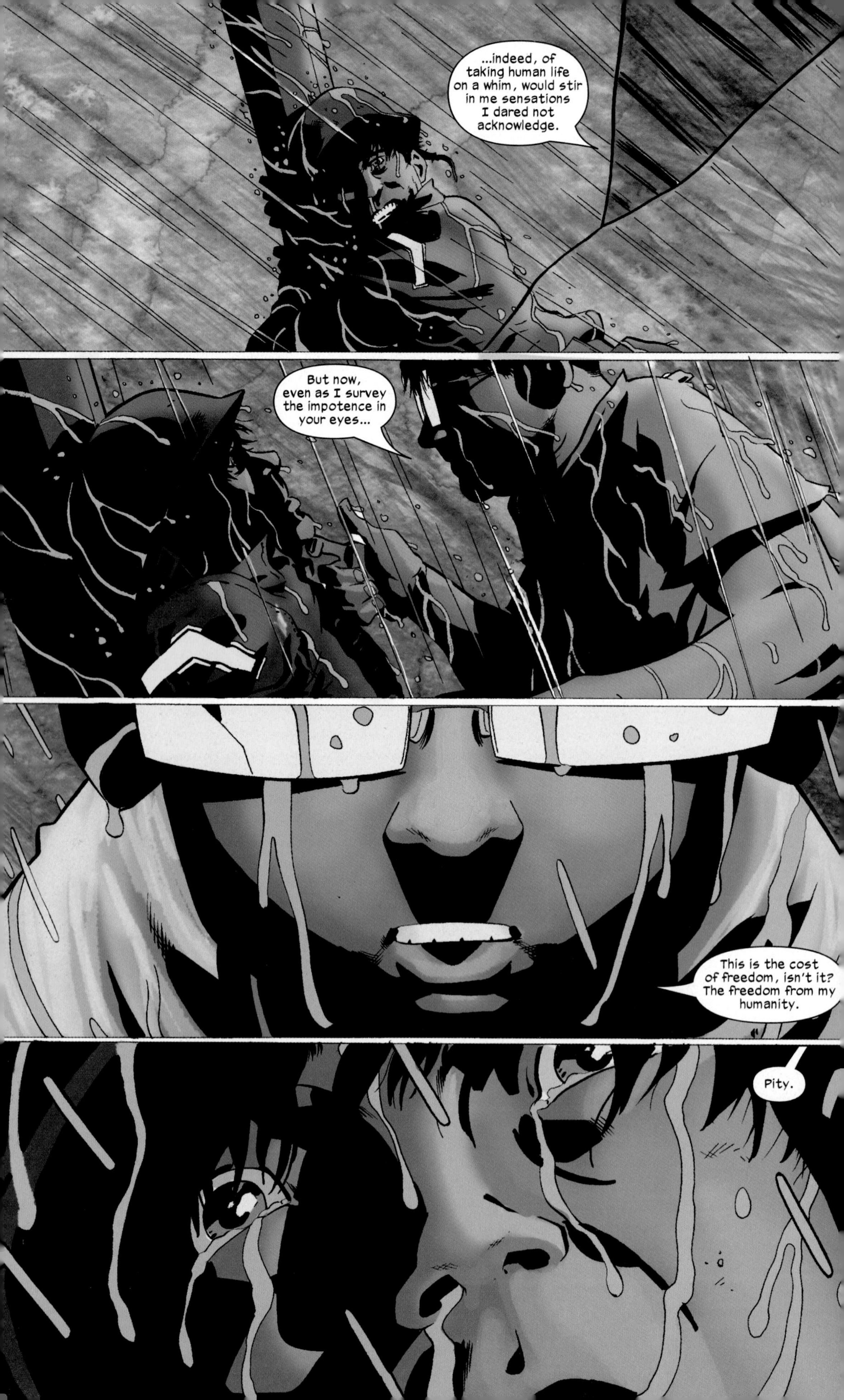
...indeed, of taking human life on a whim, would stir in me sensations I dared not acknowledge.
But now, even as I survey the impotence in your eyes...
This is the cost of freedom, isn't it? The freedom from my humanity.
Pity.

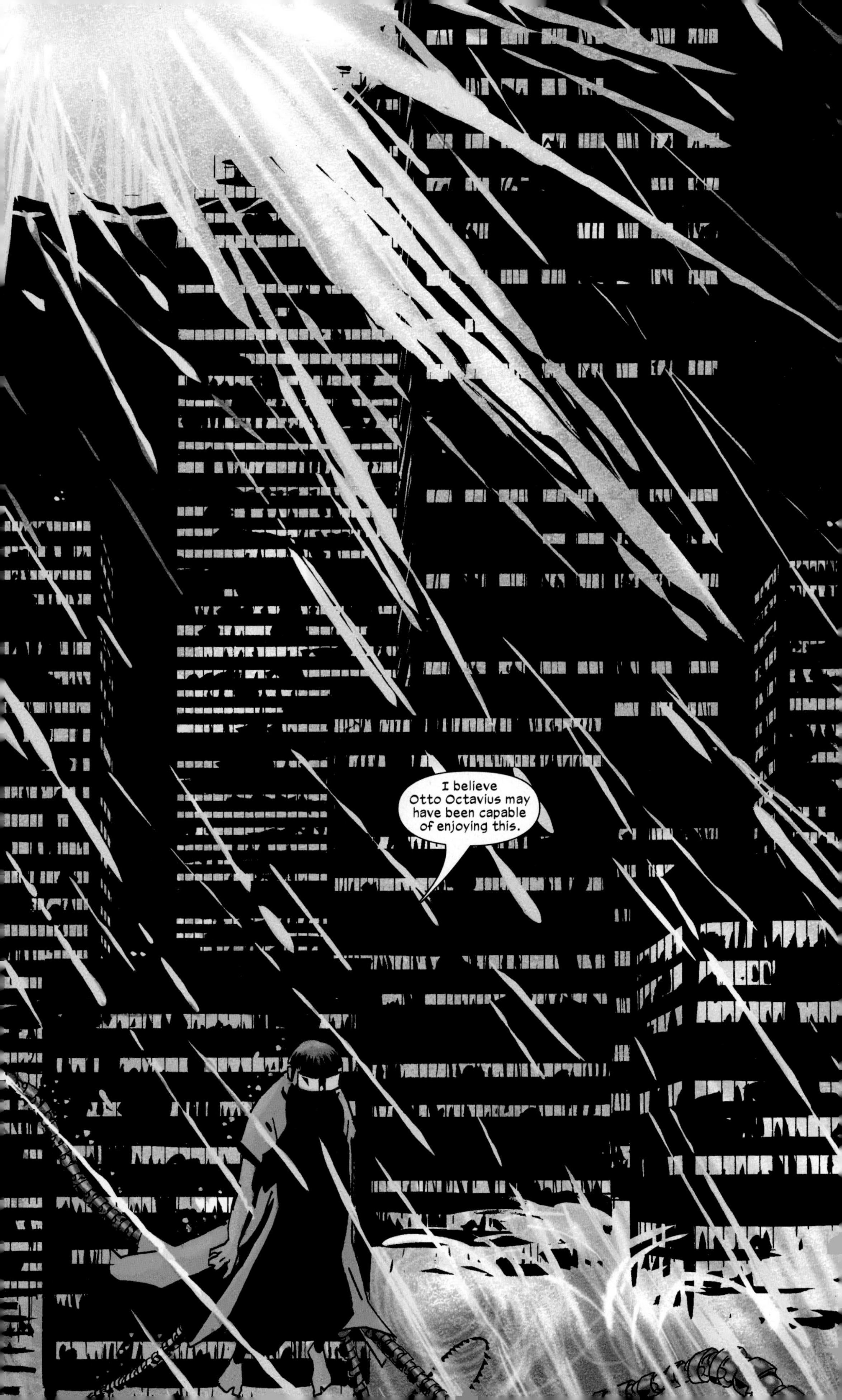
I believe Otto Octavius may have been capable of enjoying this.

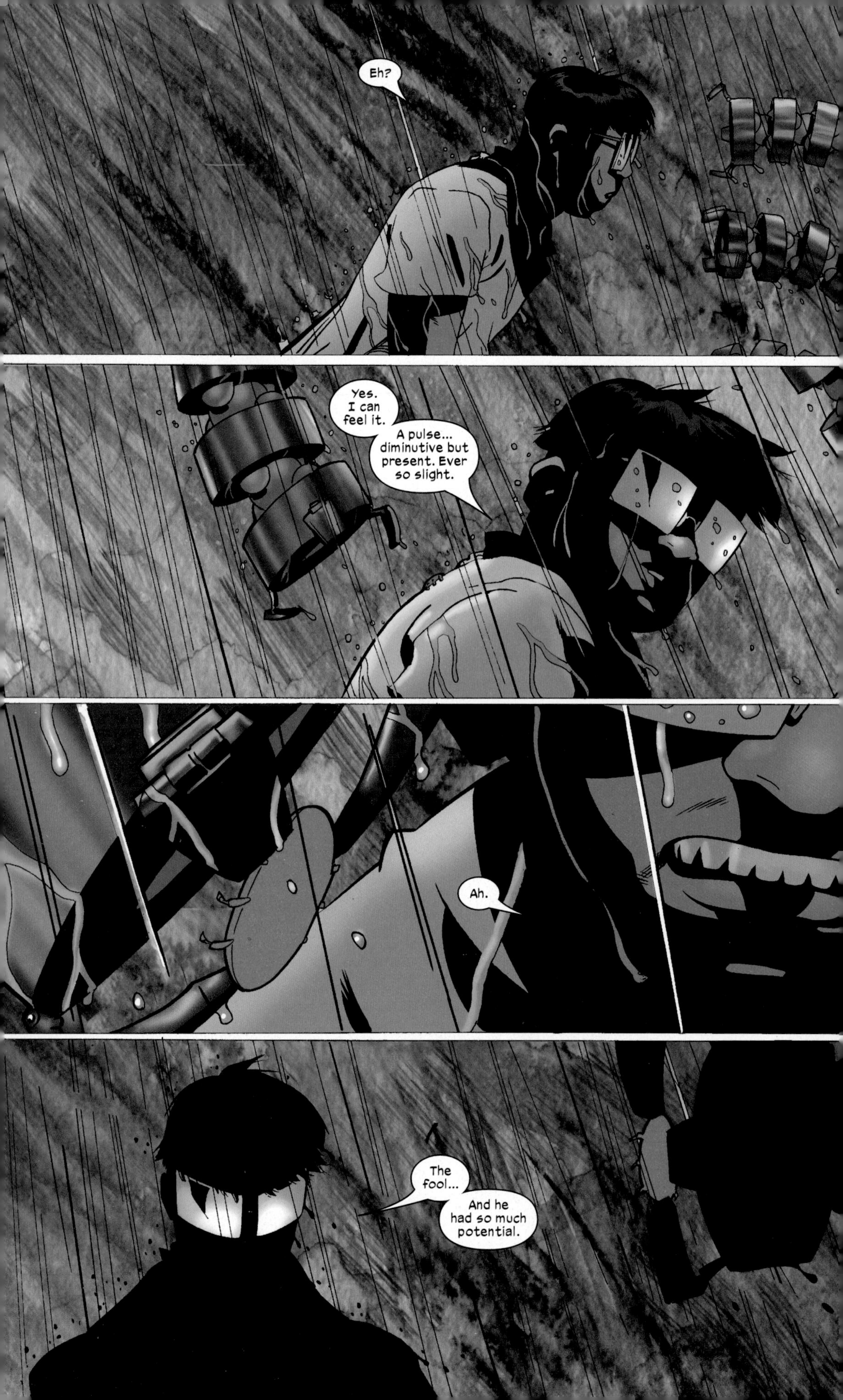
Eh?
Yes. I can feel it.
A pulse... diminutive but present. Ever so slight.
Ah.
The fool...
And he had so much potential.

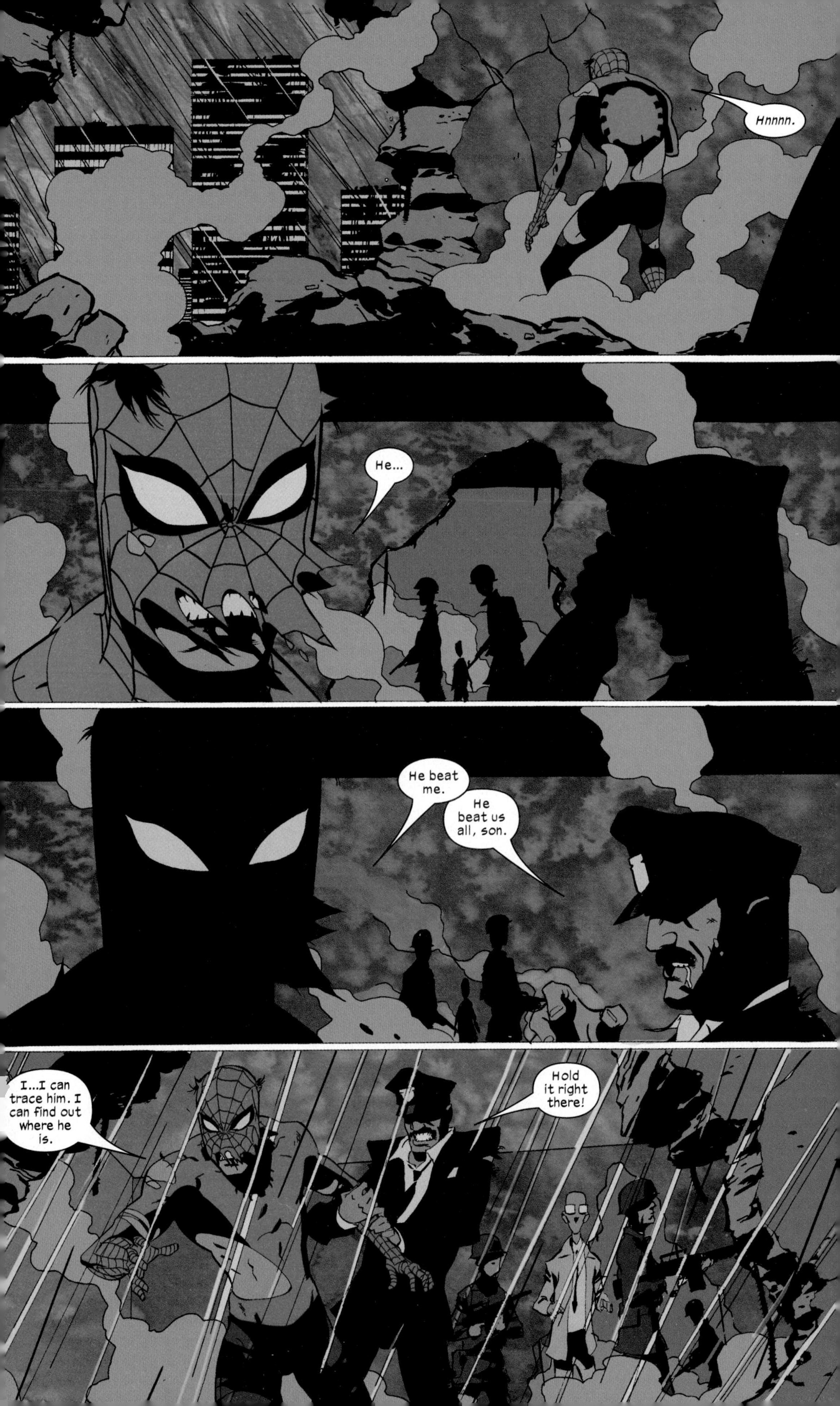
Hnnnn.
He...
He beat me.
He beat us all, son.
I...I can trace him. I can find out where he is.
Hold it right there!

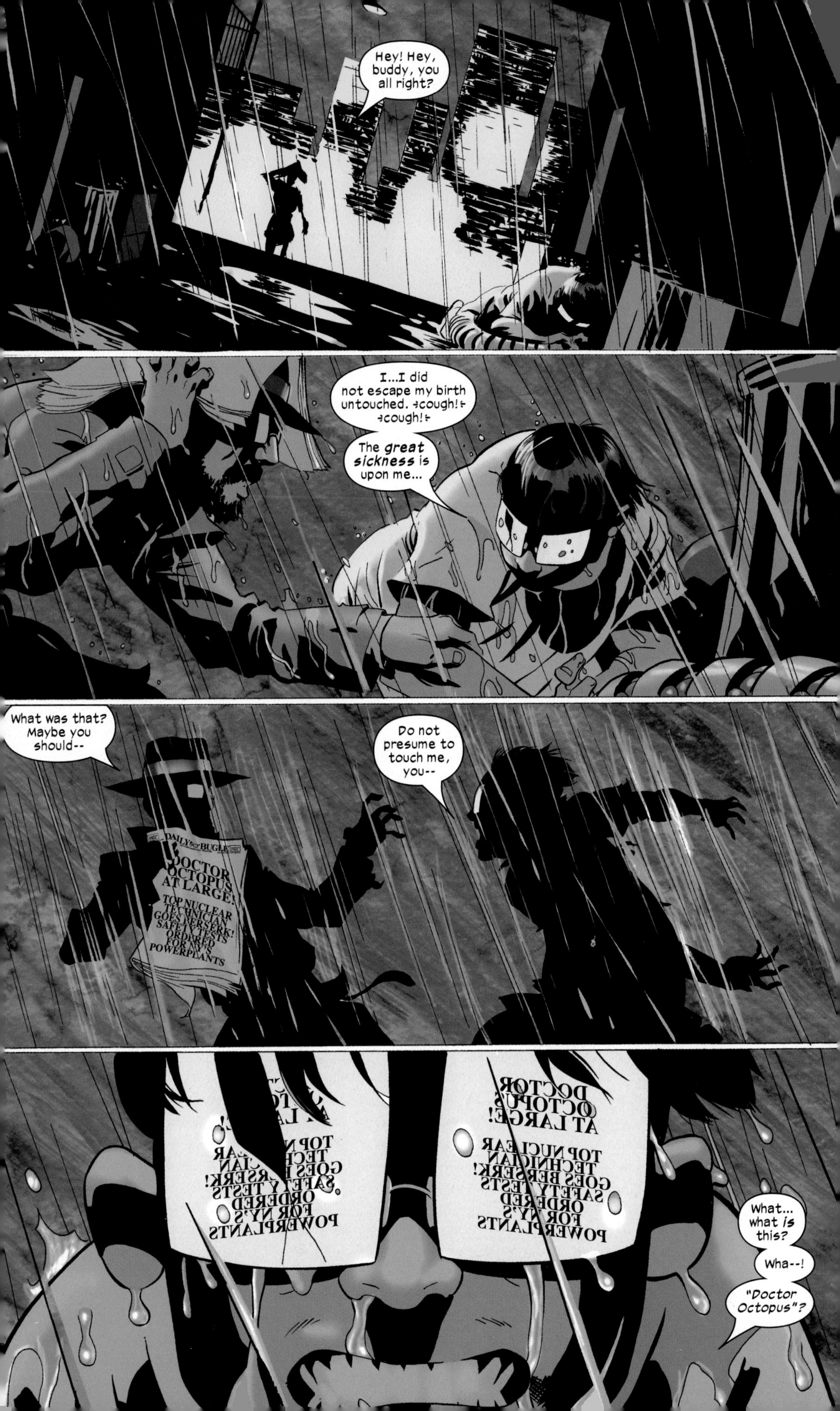
Hey! Hey, buddy, you all right?
I...I did not escape my birth untouched. ≠cough!≠ ≠cough!≠
The *great sickness* is upon me...
What was that? Maybe you should--
Do not presume to touch me, you--
DAILY BUGLE
DOCTOR OCTOPUS AT LARGE!
TOP NUCLEAR TECHNICAN GOES BERSERK! SAFETY TESTS ORDERED FOR NY'S POWERPLANTS
What... what *is* this?
Wha--!
"Doctor Octopus"?

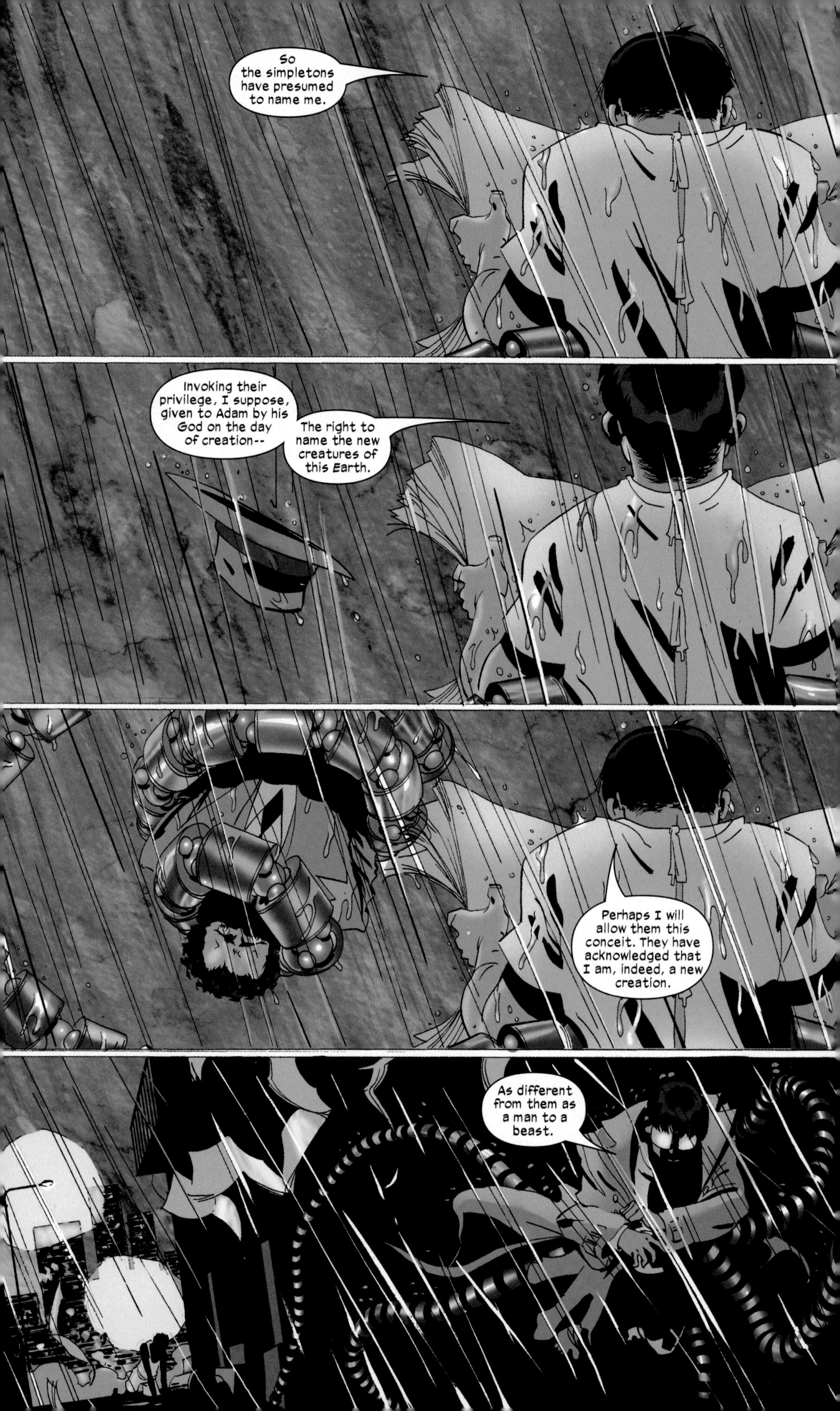
So the simpletons have presumed to name me.
Invoking their privilege, I suppose, given to Adam by his God on the day of creation--
The right to name the new creatures of this Earth.
Perhaps I will allow them this conceit. They have acknowledged that I am, indeed, a new creation.
As different from them as a man to a beast.

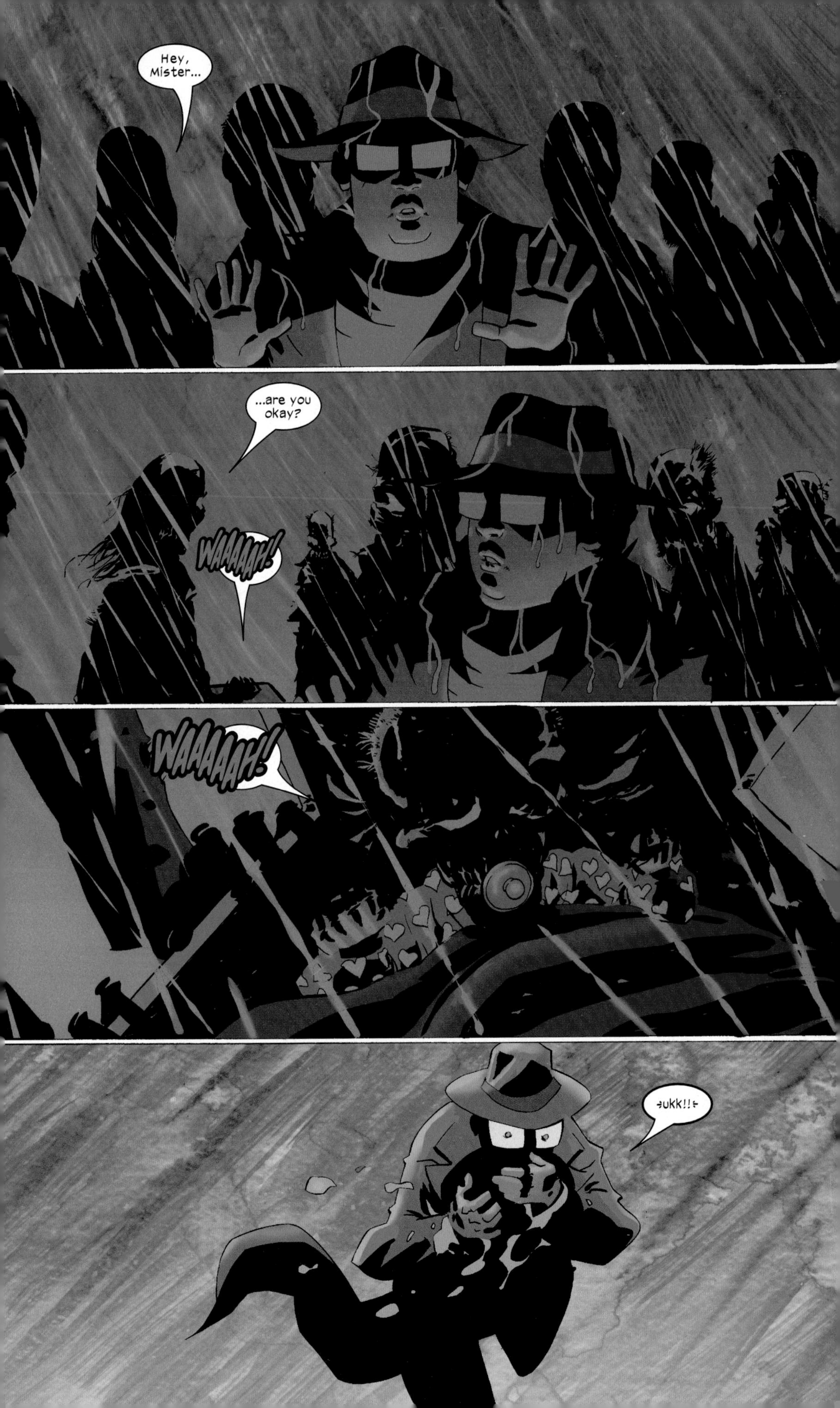
Hey, Mister...
...are you okay?
WAAAAAH!
WAAAAAH!
ukk!!

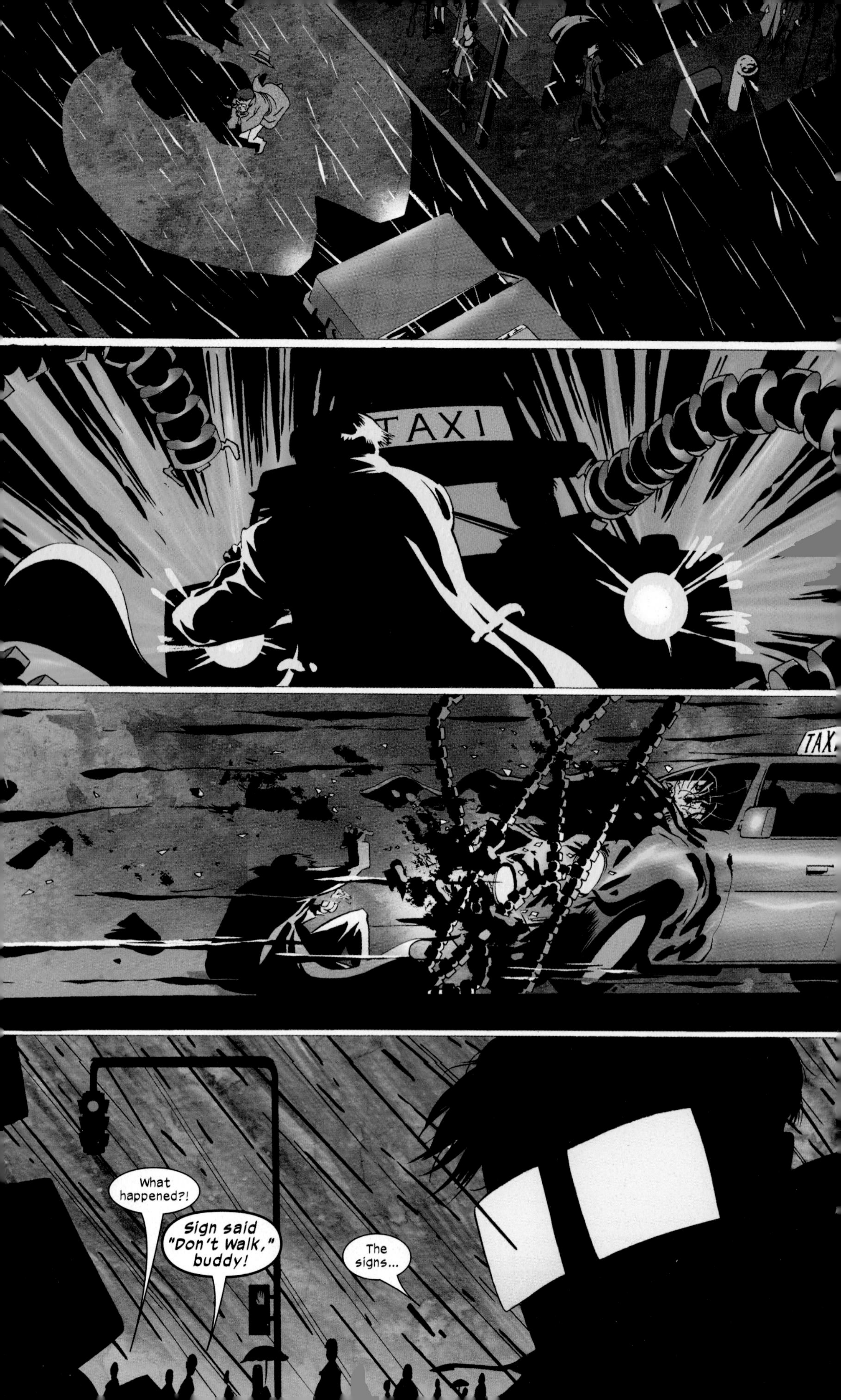
TAXI
TAX
What happened?!
Sign said "Don't Walk," buddy!
The signs...

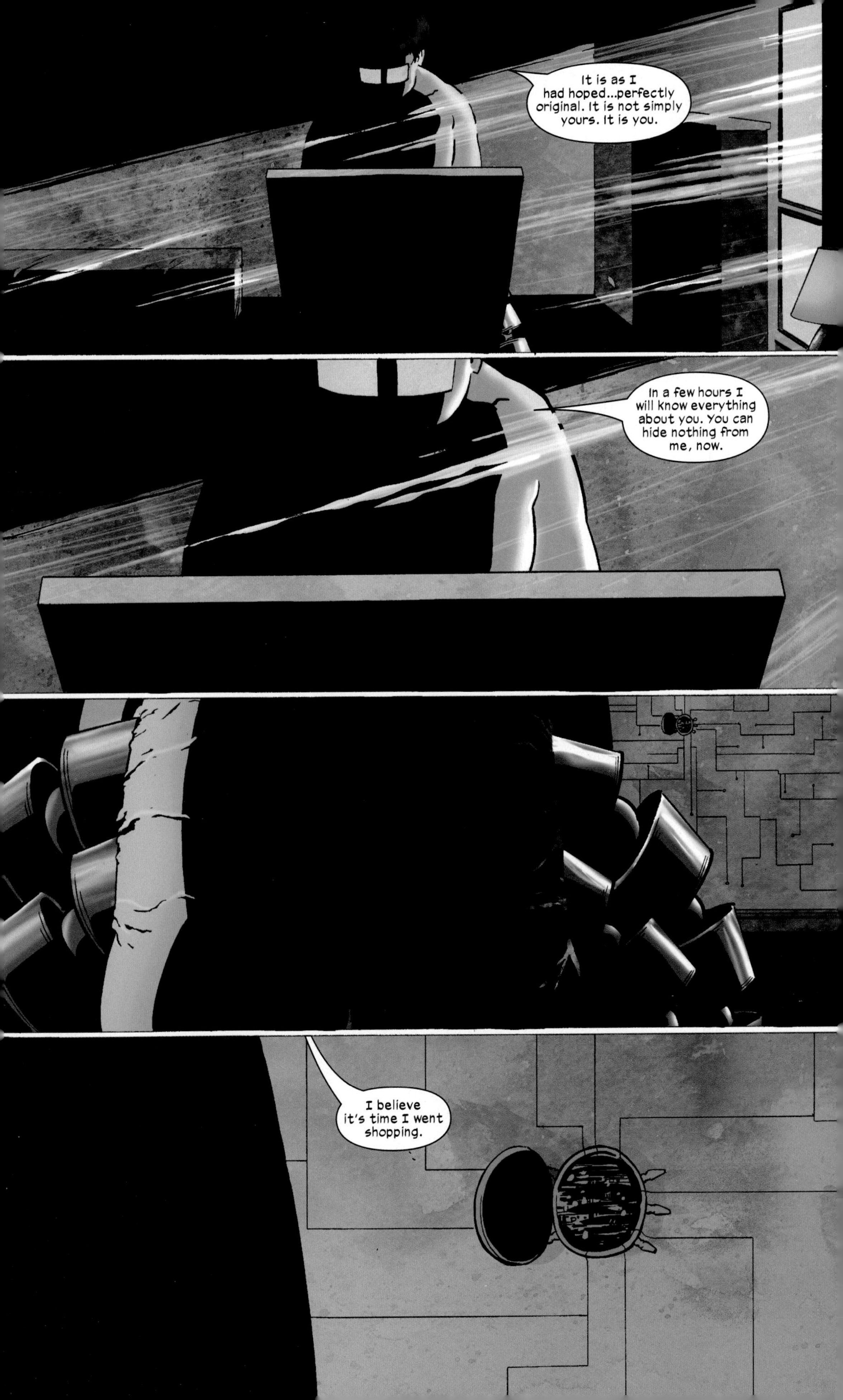
It is as I had hoped...perfectly original. It is not simply yours. It is you.
In a few hours I will know everything about you. You can hide nothing from me, now.
I believe it's time I went shopping.

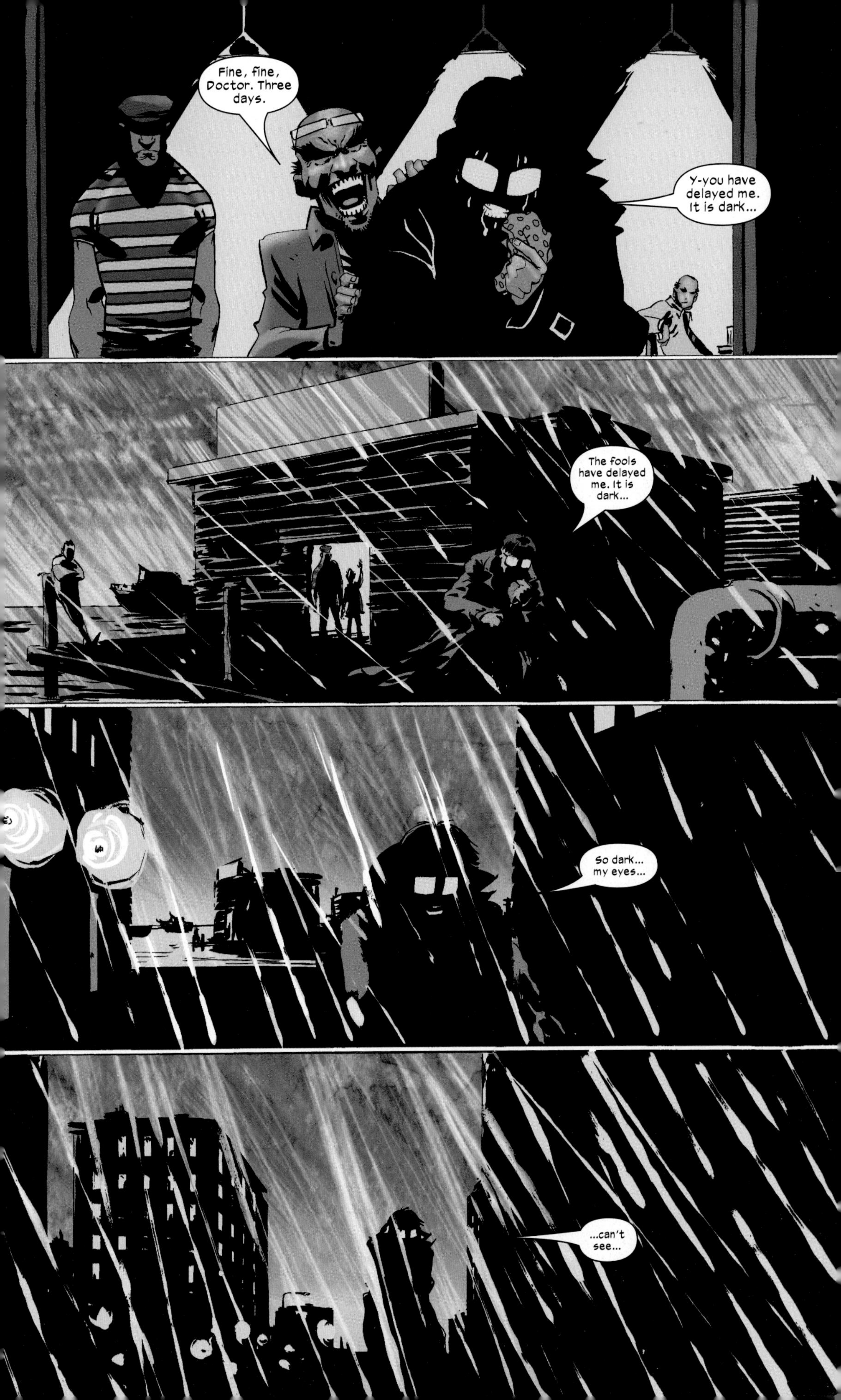
Fine, fine, Doctor. Three days.
Y-you have delayed me. It is dark...
The fools have delayed me. It is dark...
So dark... my eyes...
...can't see...

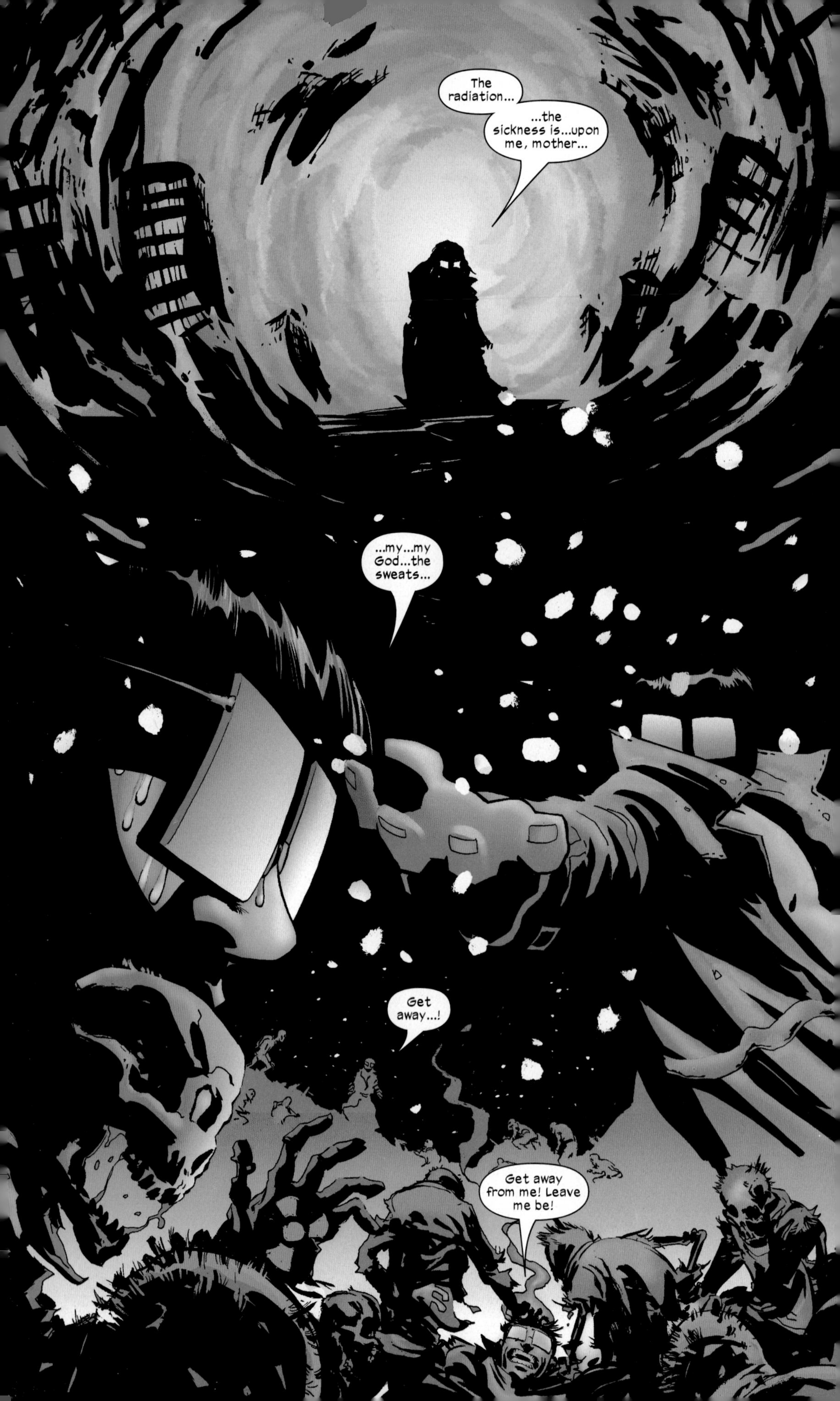

The radiation...
...the sickness is...upon me, mother...
...my...my God...the sweats...
Get away...!
Get away from me! Leave me be!

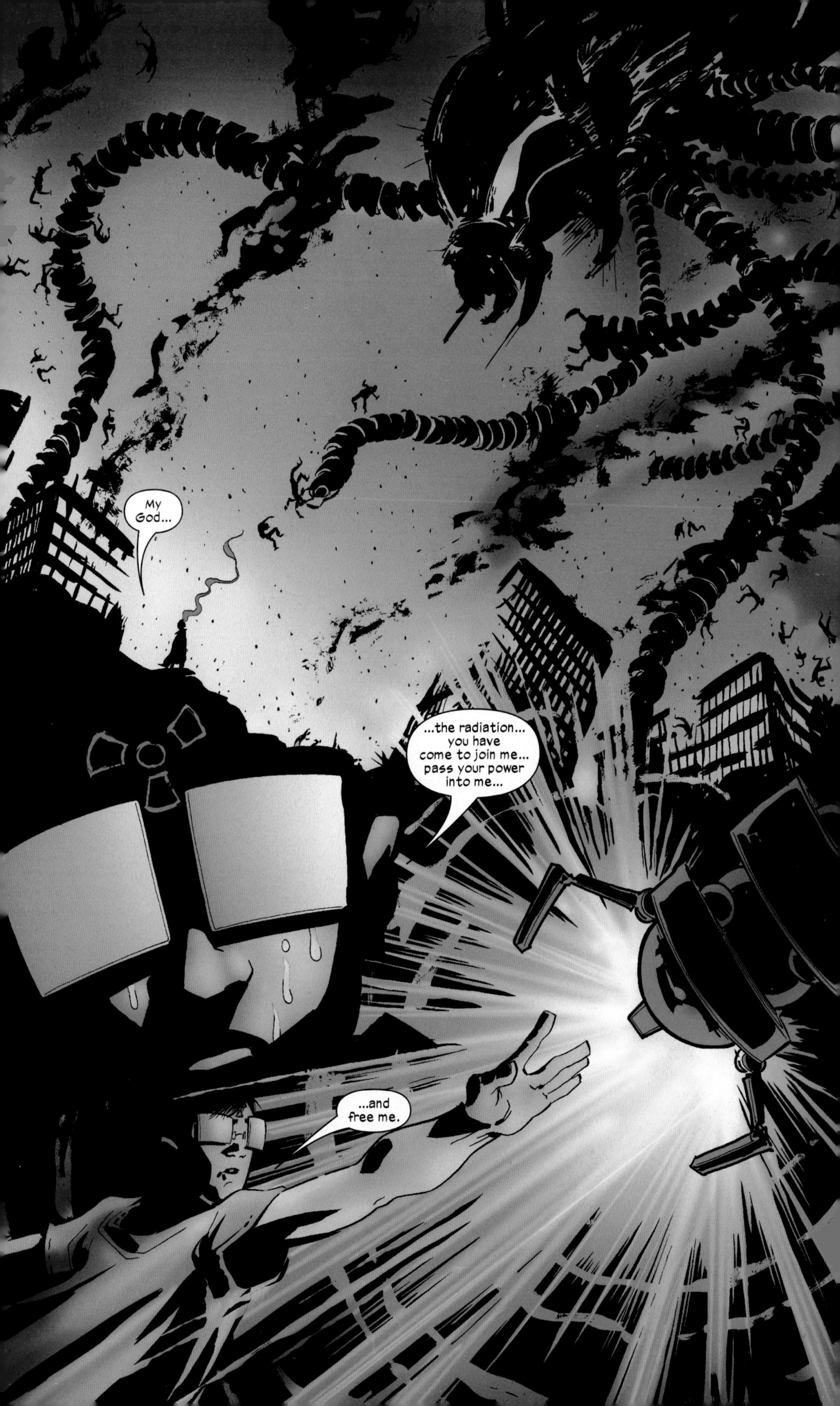
My God...
...the radiation... you have come to join me... pass your power into me...
...and free me.

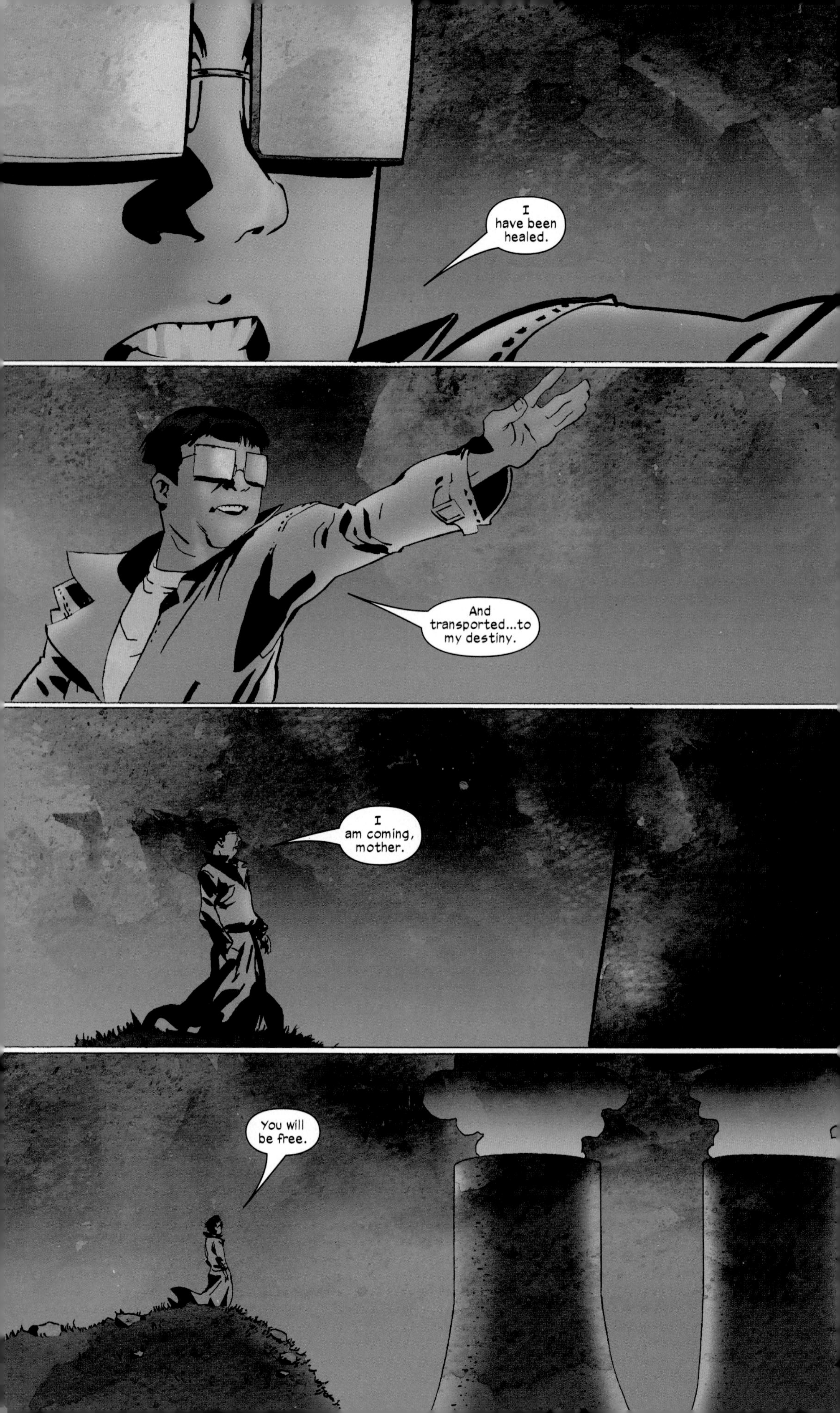
I have been healed.
And transported...to my destiny.
I am coming, mother.
You will be free.

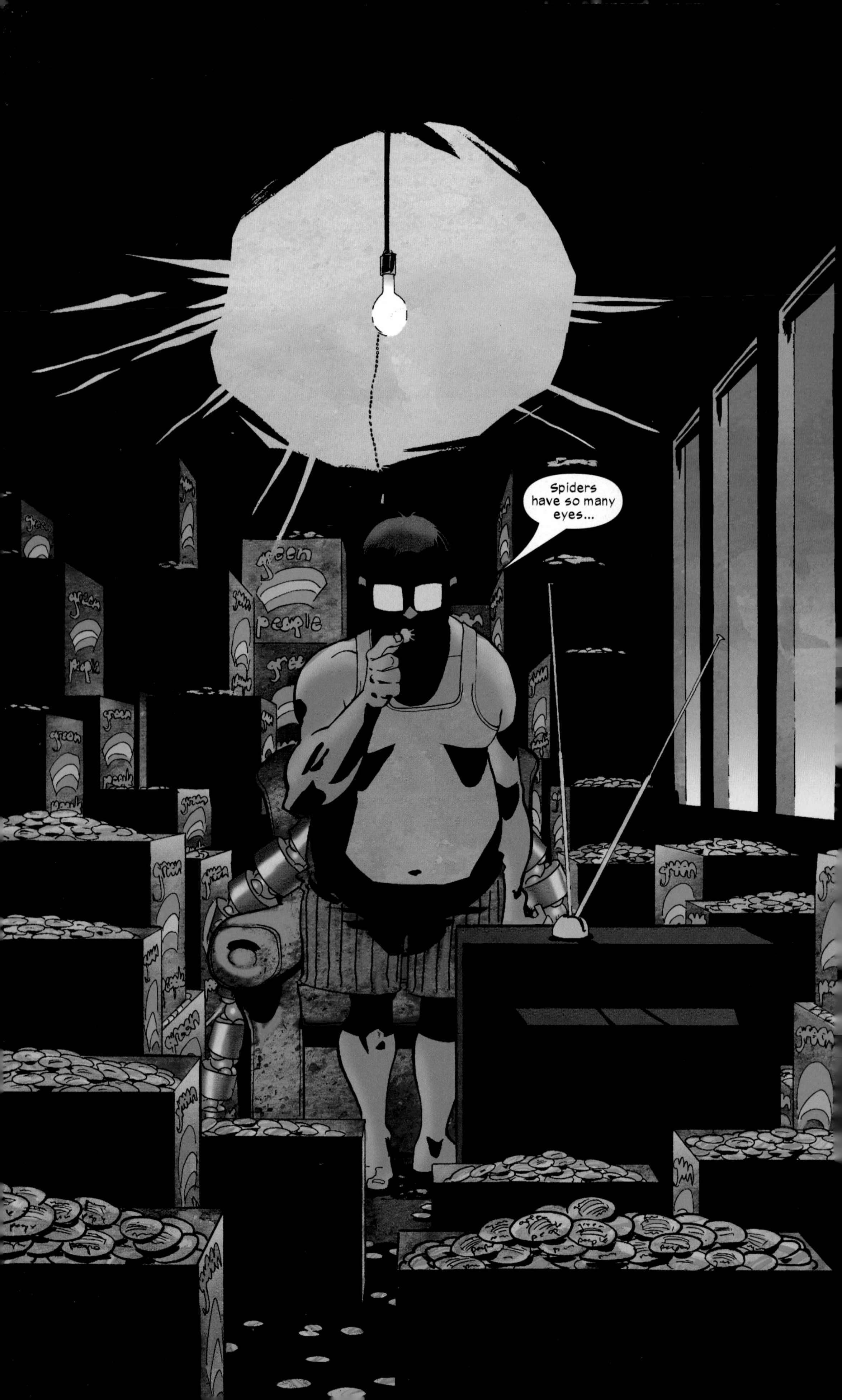
Spiders have so many eyes...

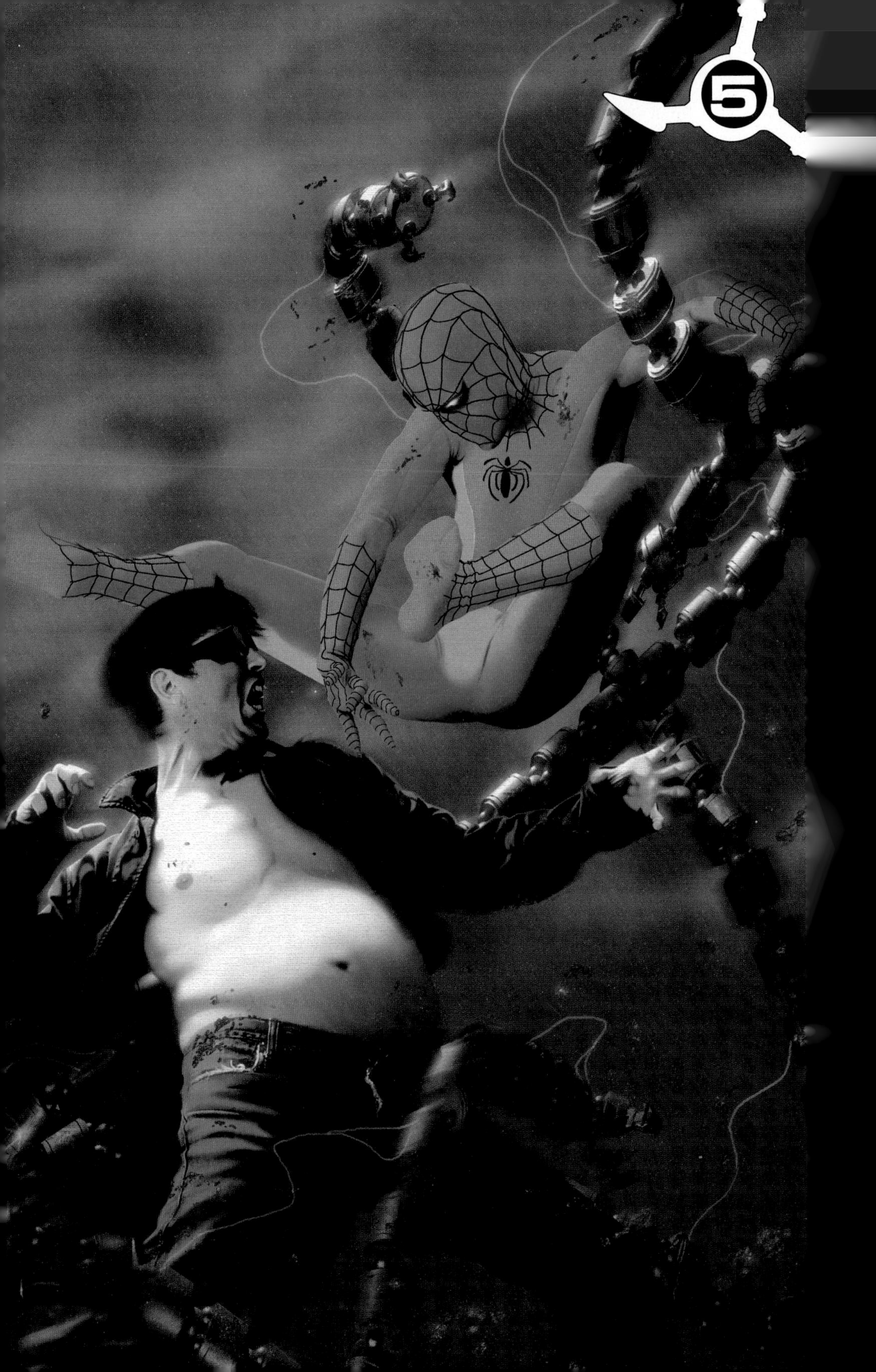
5

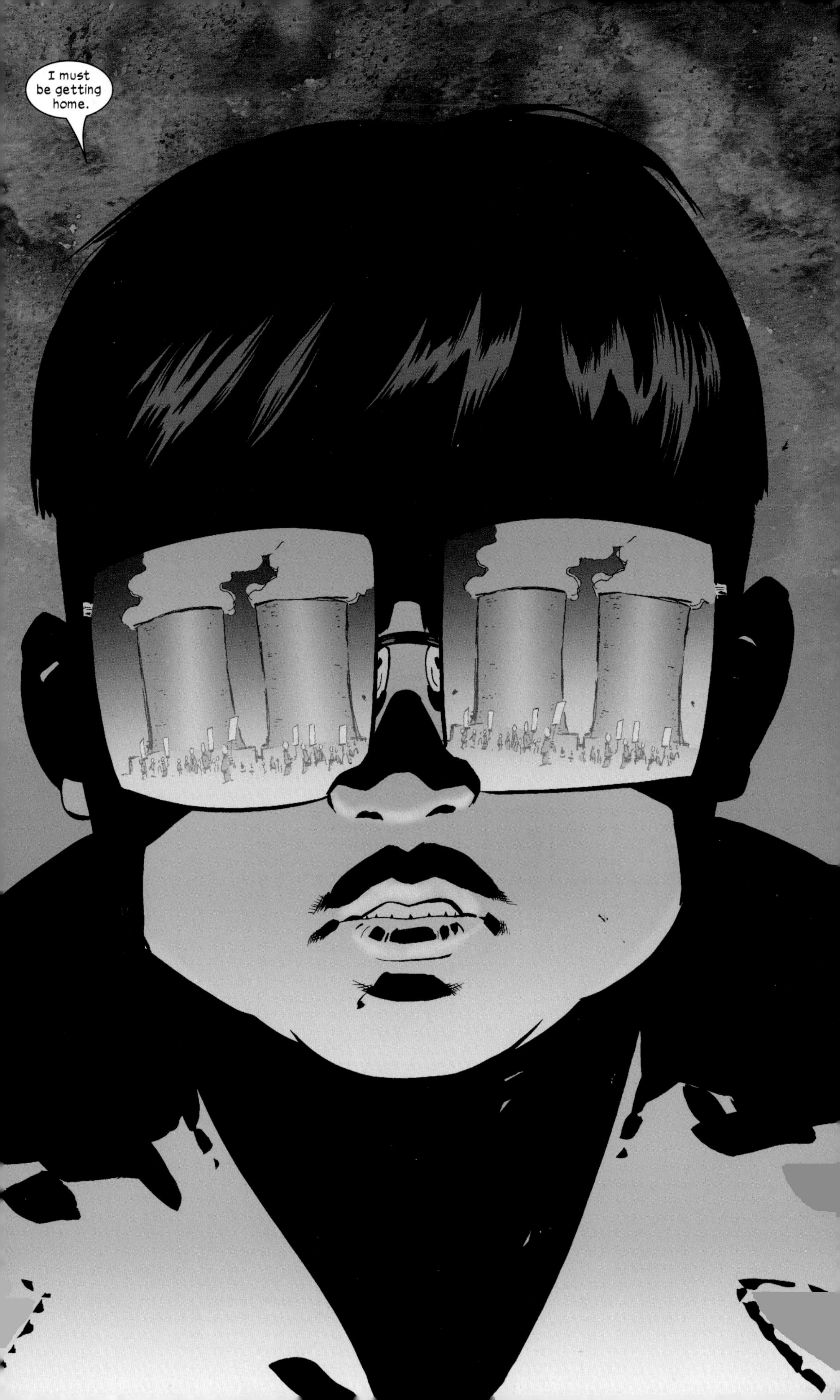
I must be getting home.

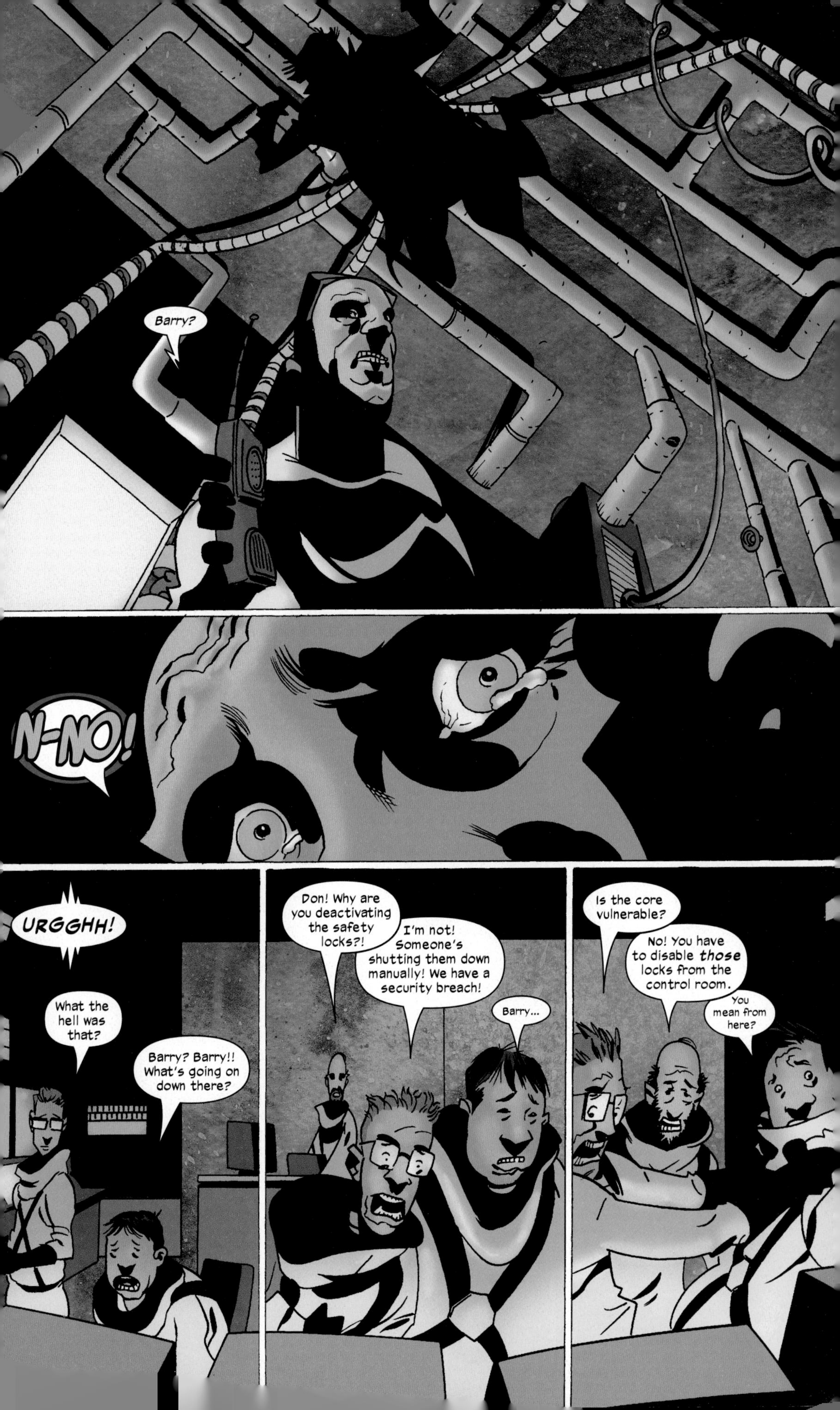
Barry?
N-NO!
URGGHH!
What the hell was that?
Barry? Barry!! What's going on down there?
Don! Why are you deactivating the safety locks?!
I'm not! Someone's shutting them down manually! We have a security breach!
Barry...
Is the core vulnerable?
No! You have to disable *those* locks from the control room.
You mean from here?

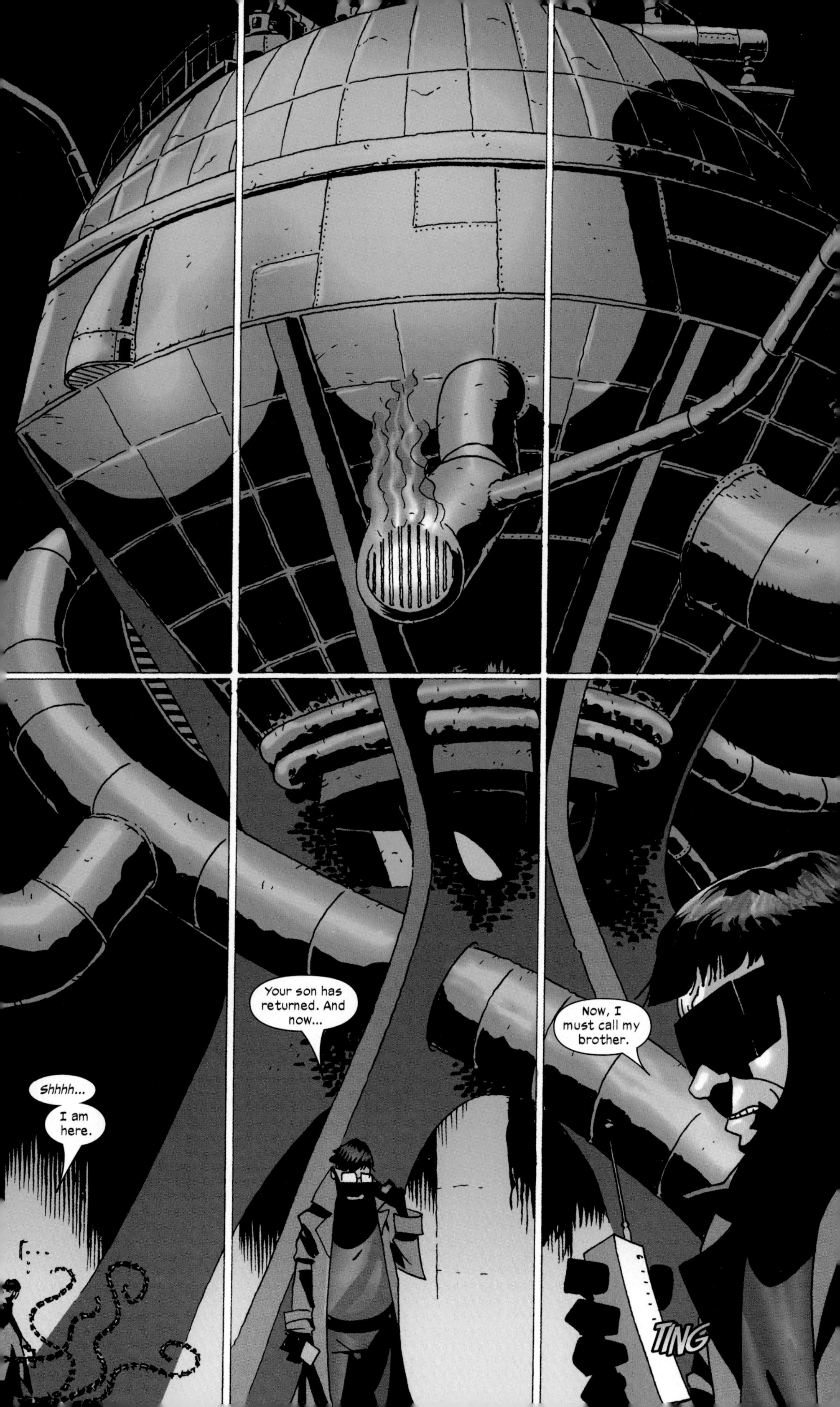
Shhhh...
I am here.
Your son has returned. And now...
Now, I must call my brother.
TING

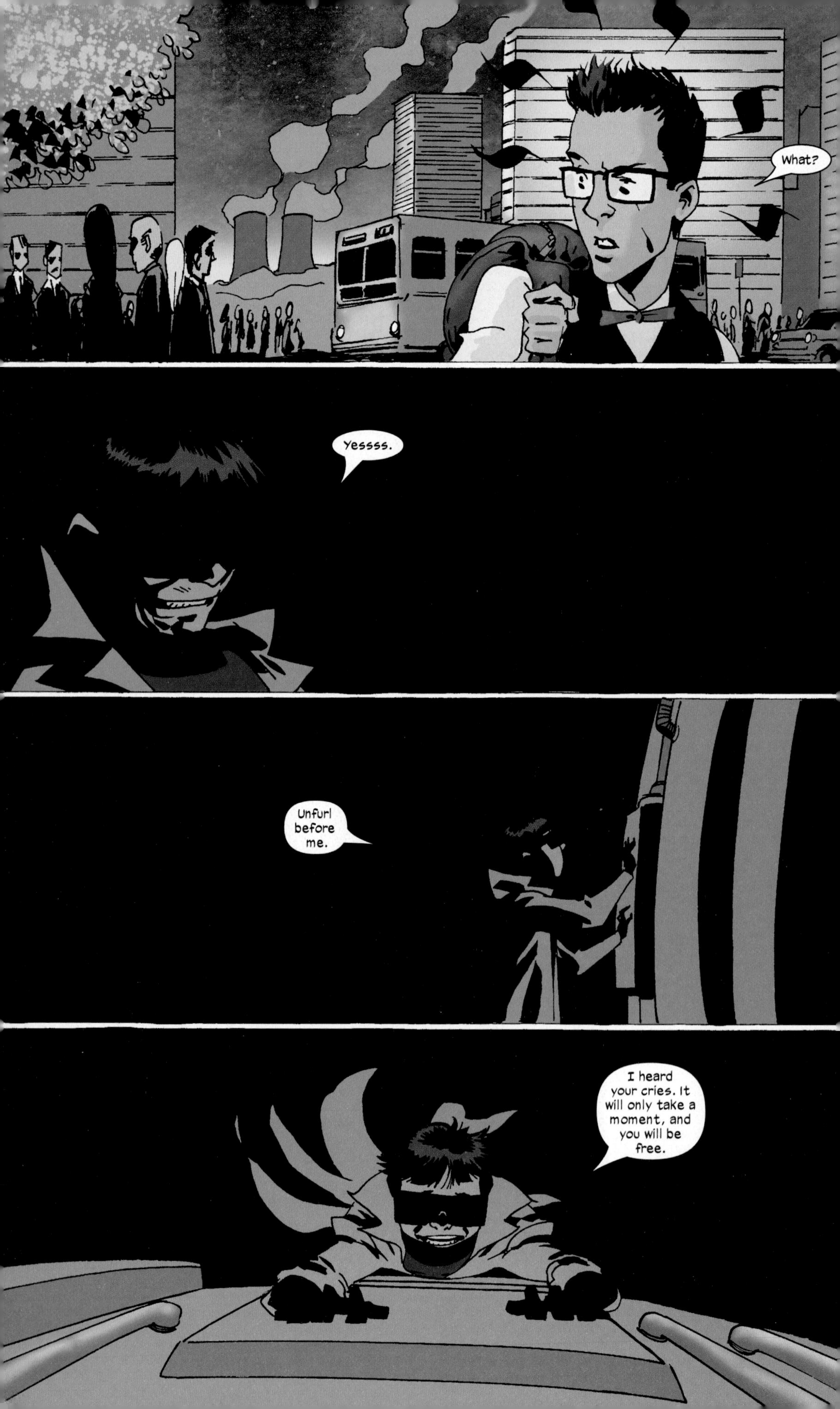
What?
Yessss.
Unfurl before me.
I heard your cries. It will only take a moment, and you will be free.

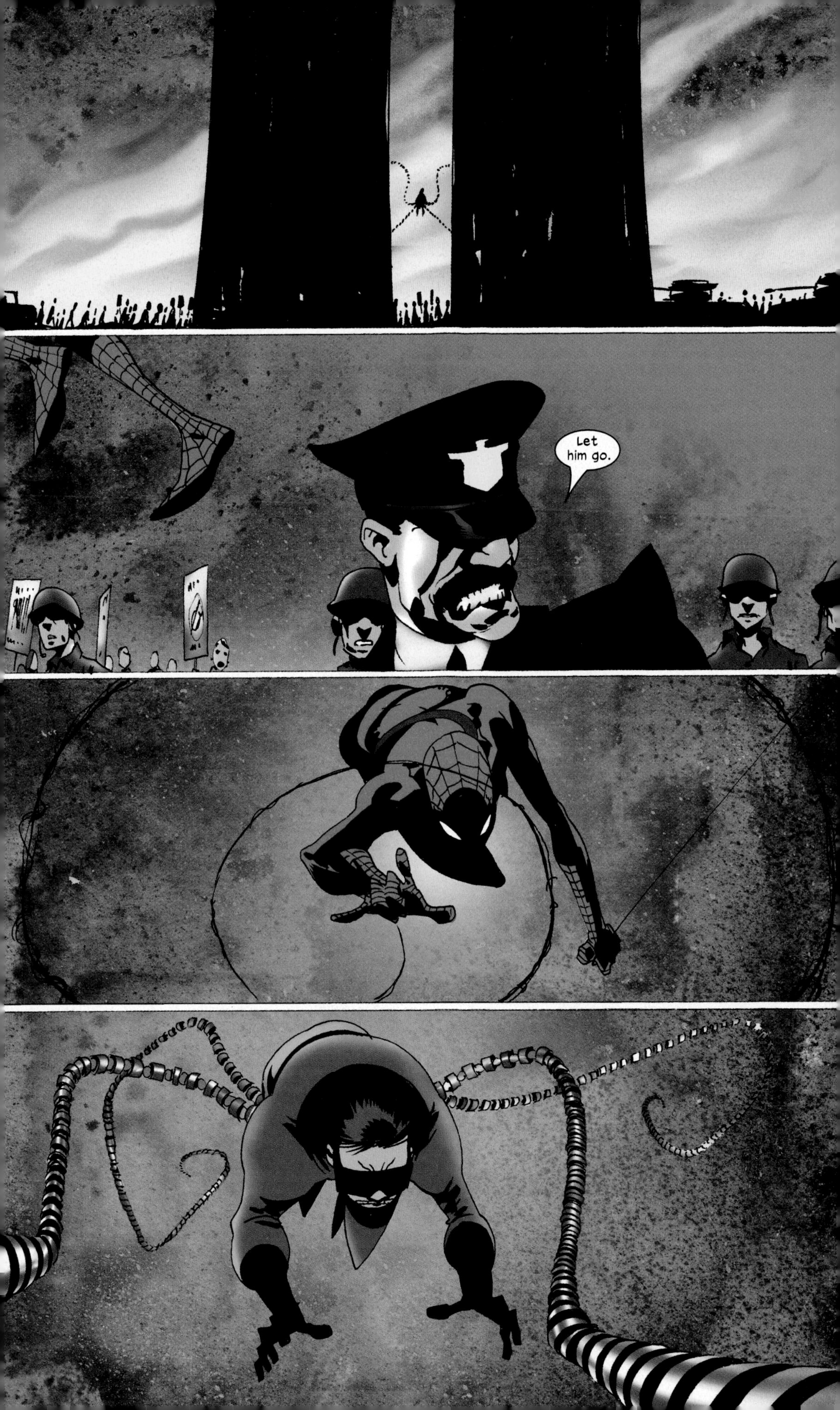
Let him go.

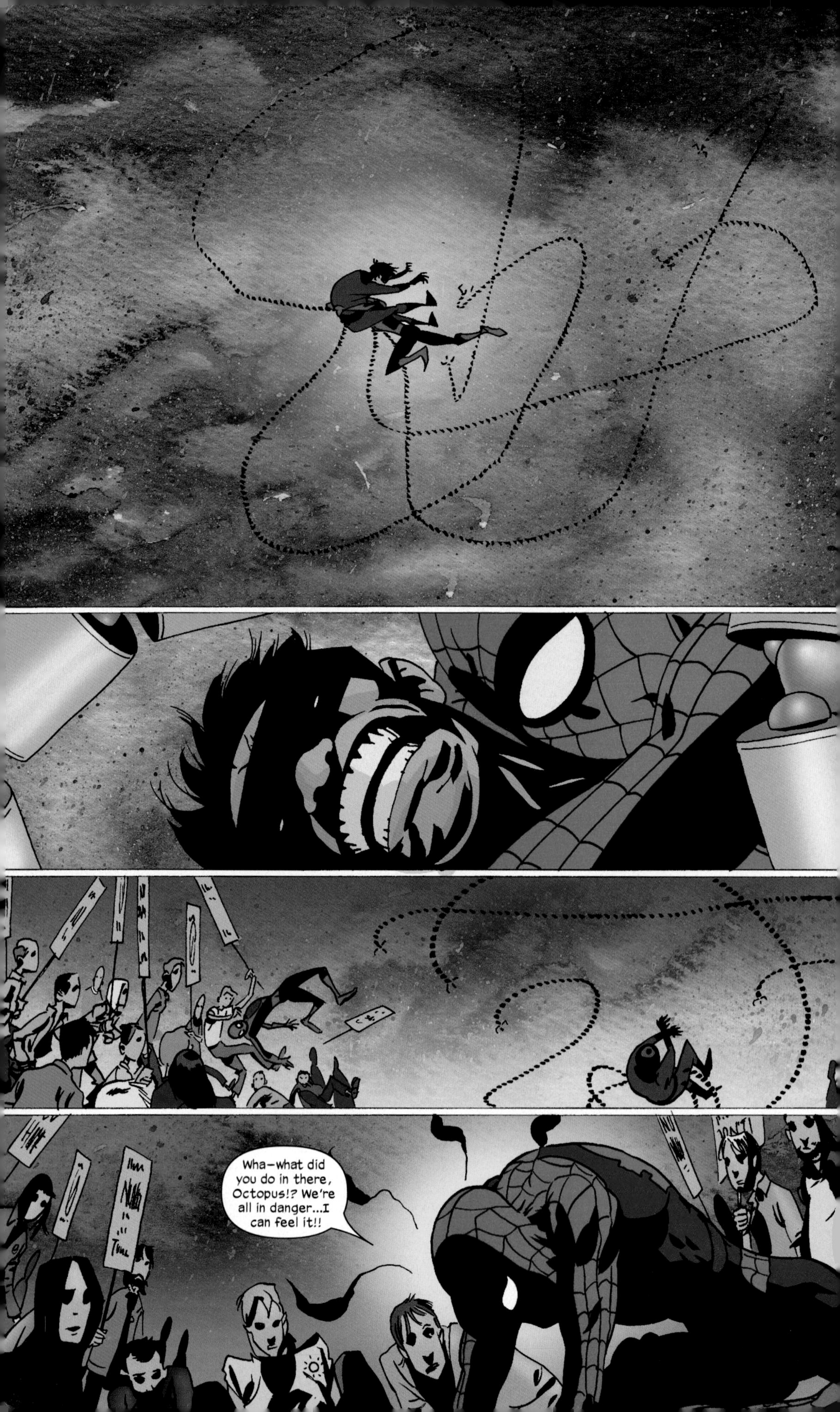
Wha–what did you do in there, Octopus!? We're all in danger...I can feel it!!

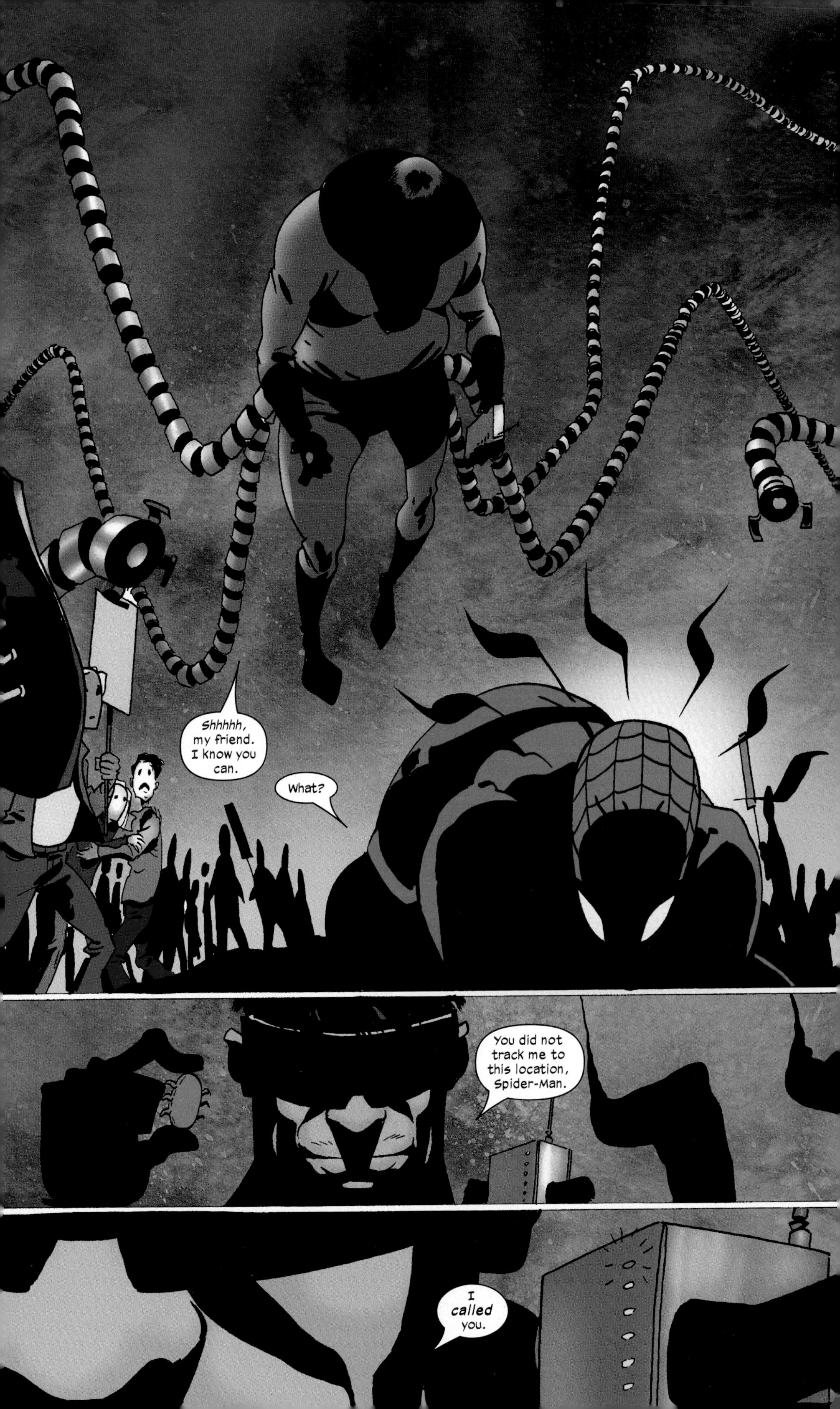
Shhhhh,
my friend.
I know you
can.
What?
You did not
track me to
this location,
Spider-Man.
I
called
you.

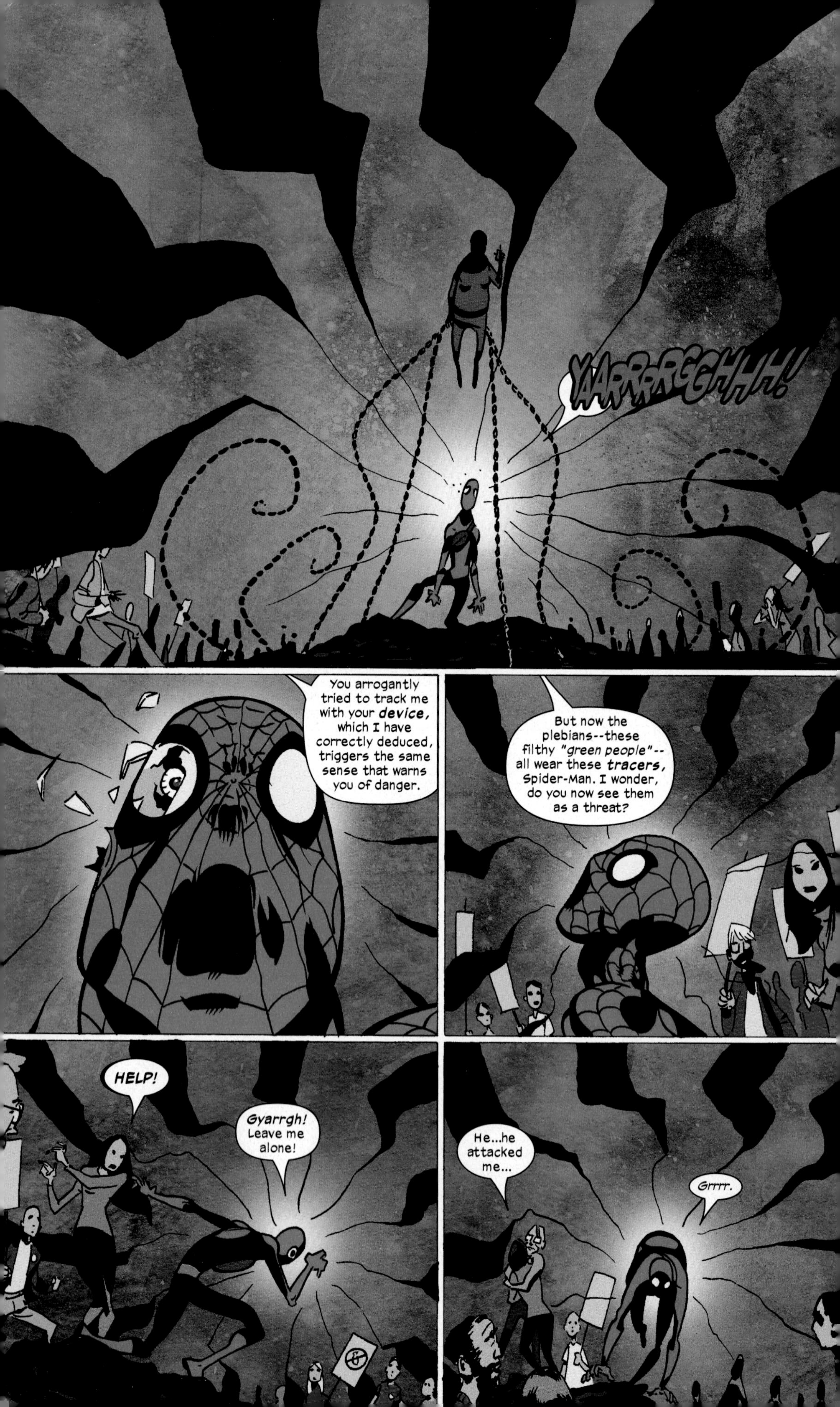
YAARRRRGGHHH!
You arrogantly tried to track me with your *device,* which I have correctly deduced, triggers the same sense that warns you of danger.
But now the plebians--these filthy *"green people"*--all wear these *tracers,* Spider-Man. I wonder, do you now see them as a threat?
HELP!
Gyarrgh! Leave me alone!
He...he attacked me...
Grrrr.

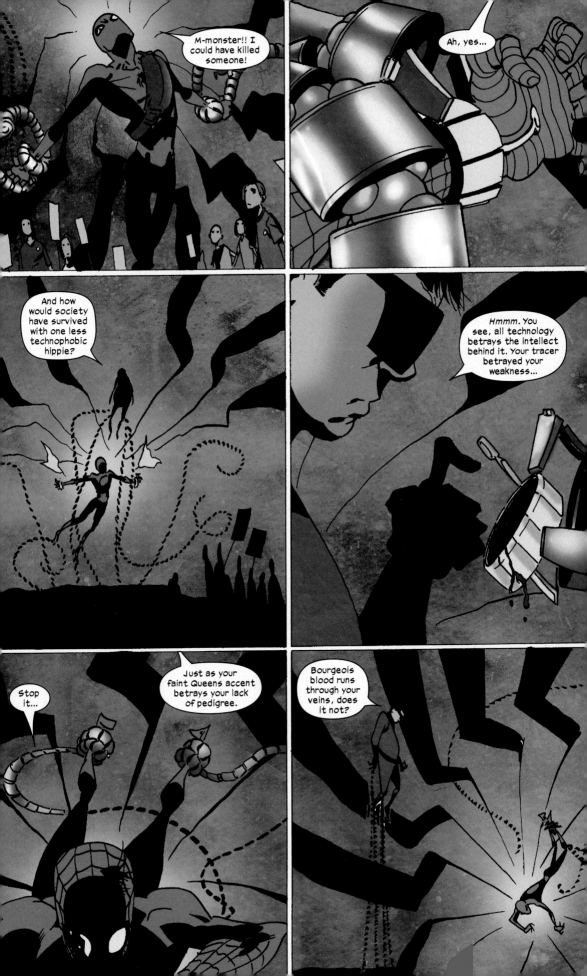

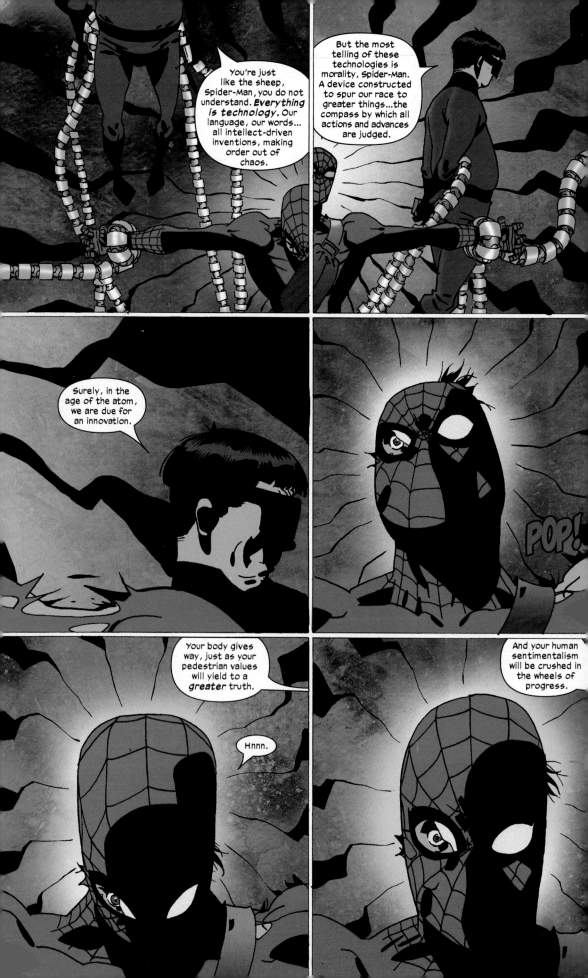

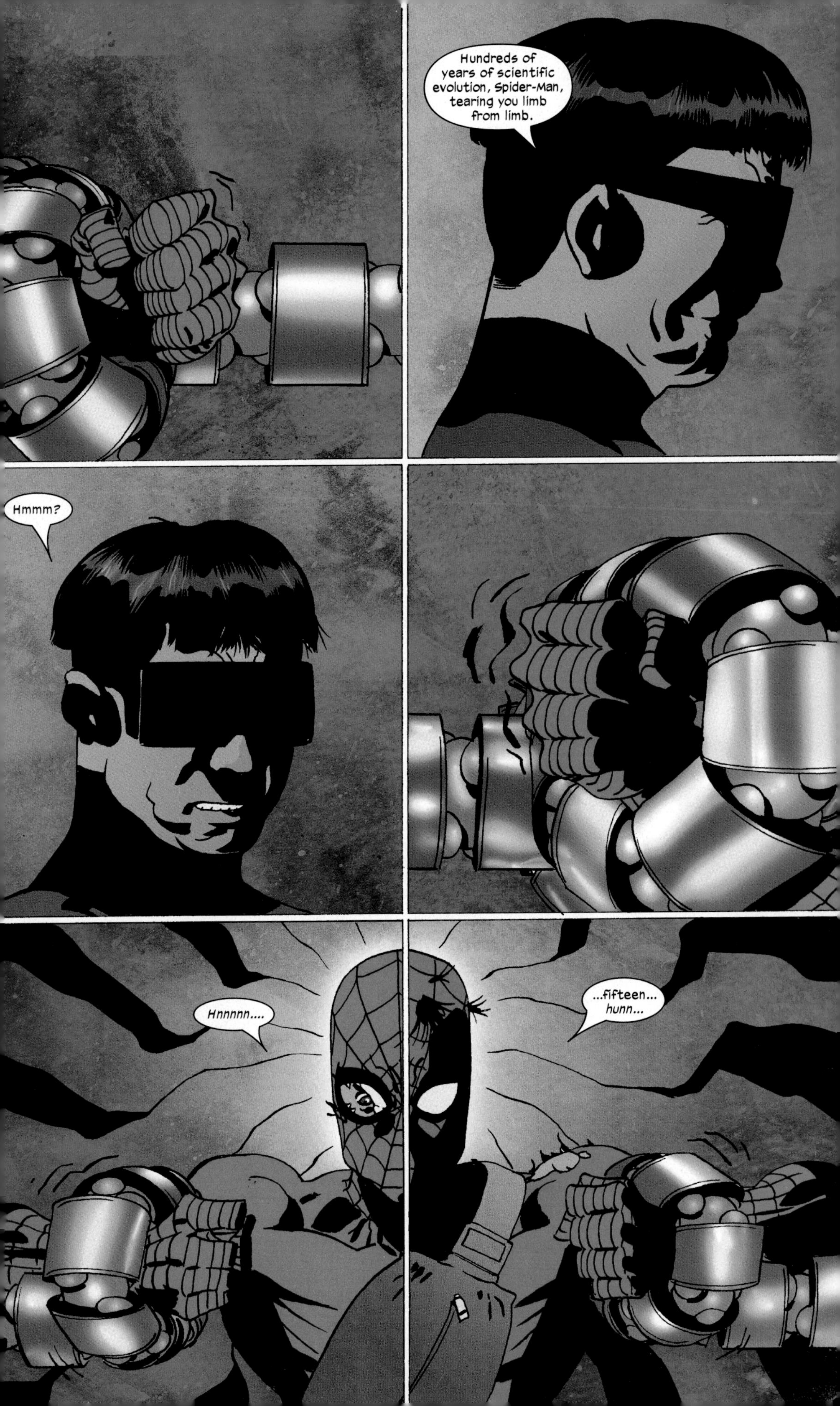
Hundreds of years of scientific evolution, Spider-Man, tearing you limb from limb.
Hmmm?
Hnnnnn....
...fifteen... hunn...

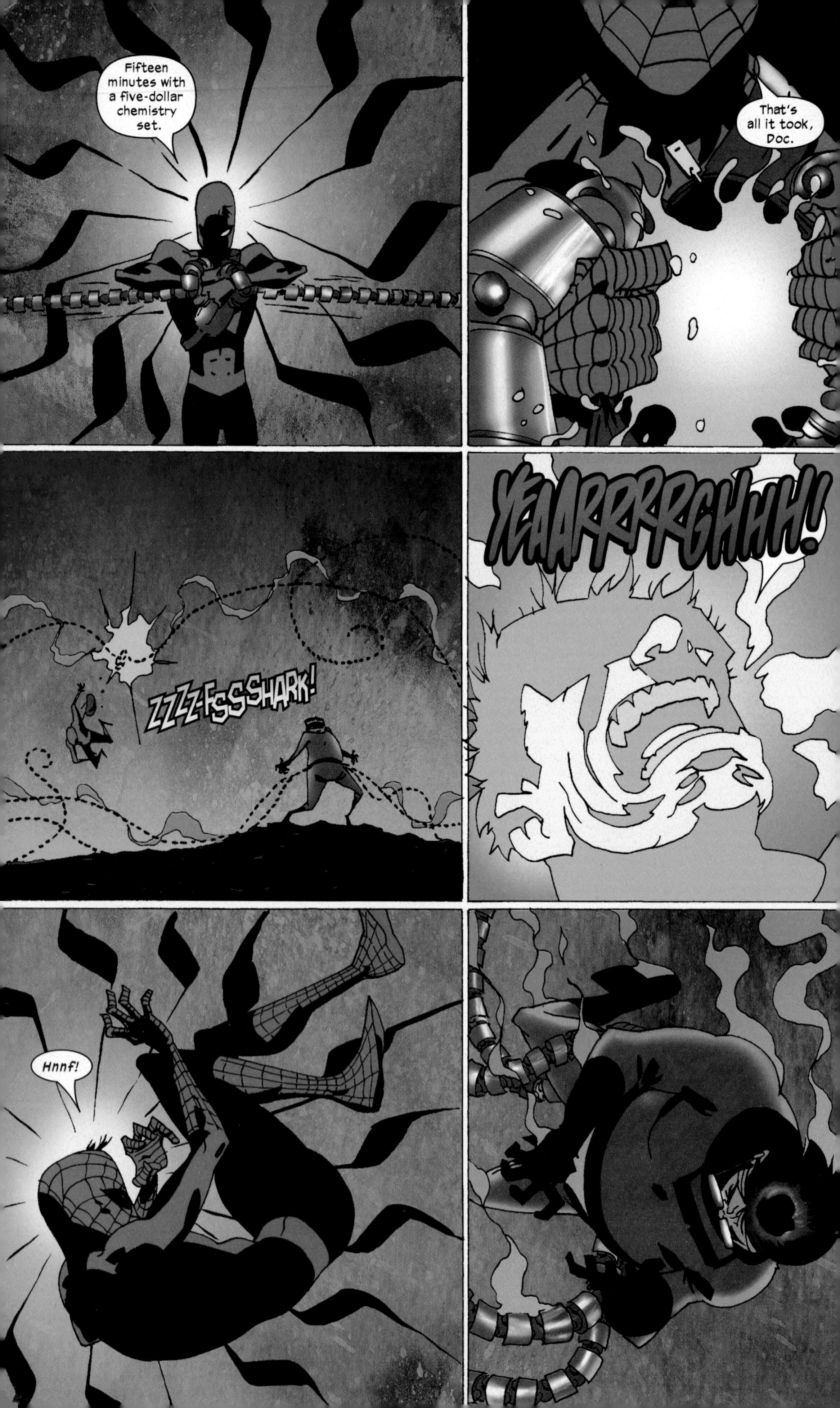
Fifteen minutes with a five-dollar chemistry set.
That's all it took, Doc.
ZZZZ-FSSSHARK!
YEAARRRRGHHH!
Hnnf!

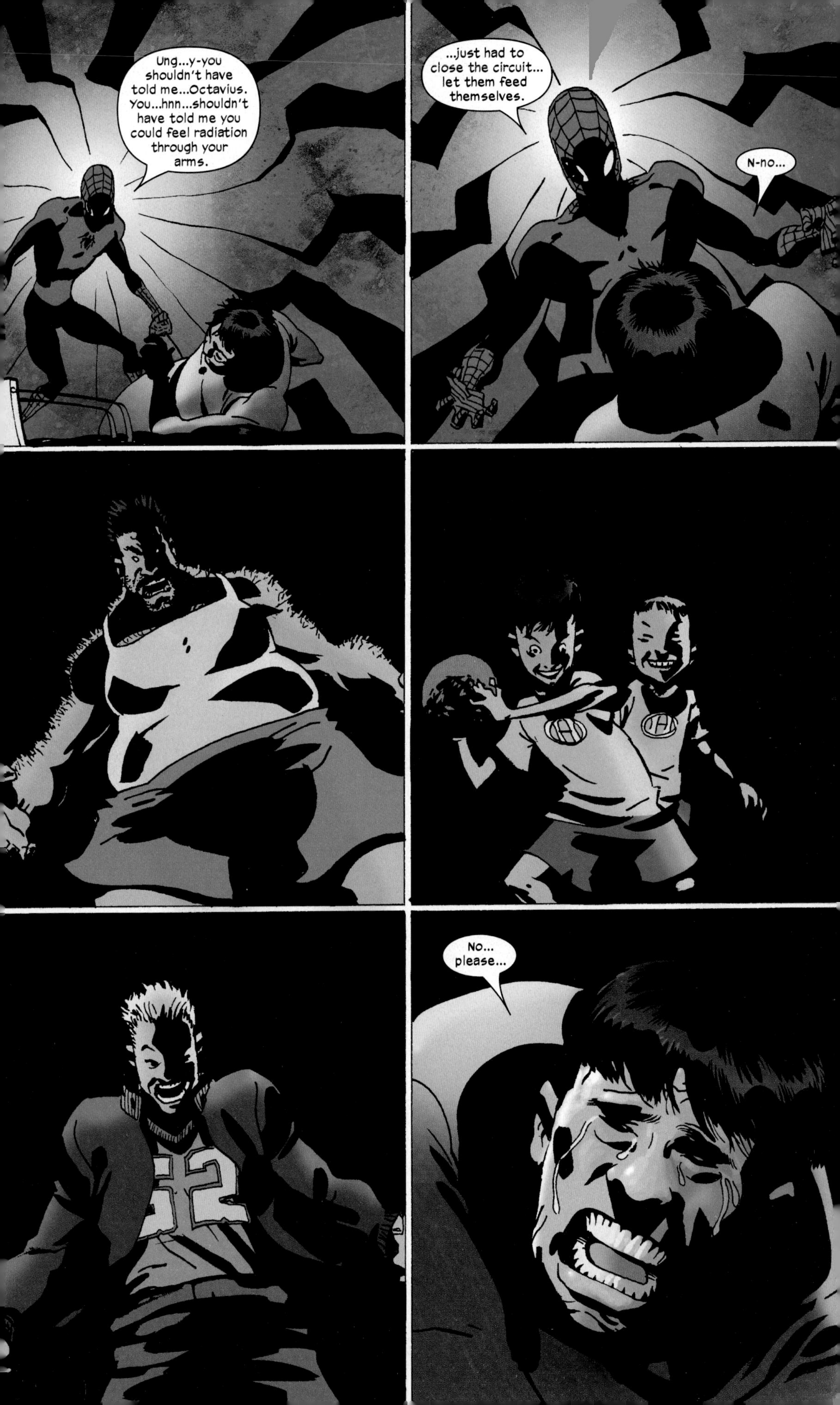
Ung...y-you shouldn't have told me...Octavius. You...hnn...shouldn't have told me you could feel radiation through your arms.
...just had to close the circuit... let them feed themselves.
N-no...
No... please...

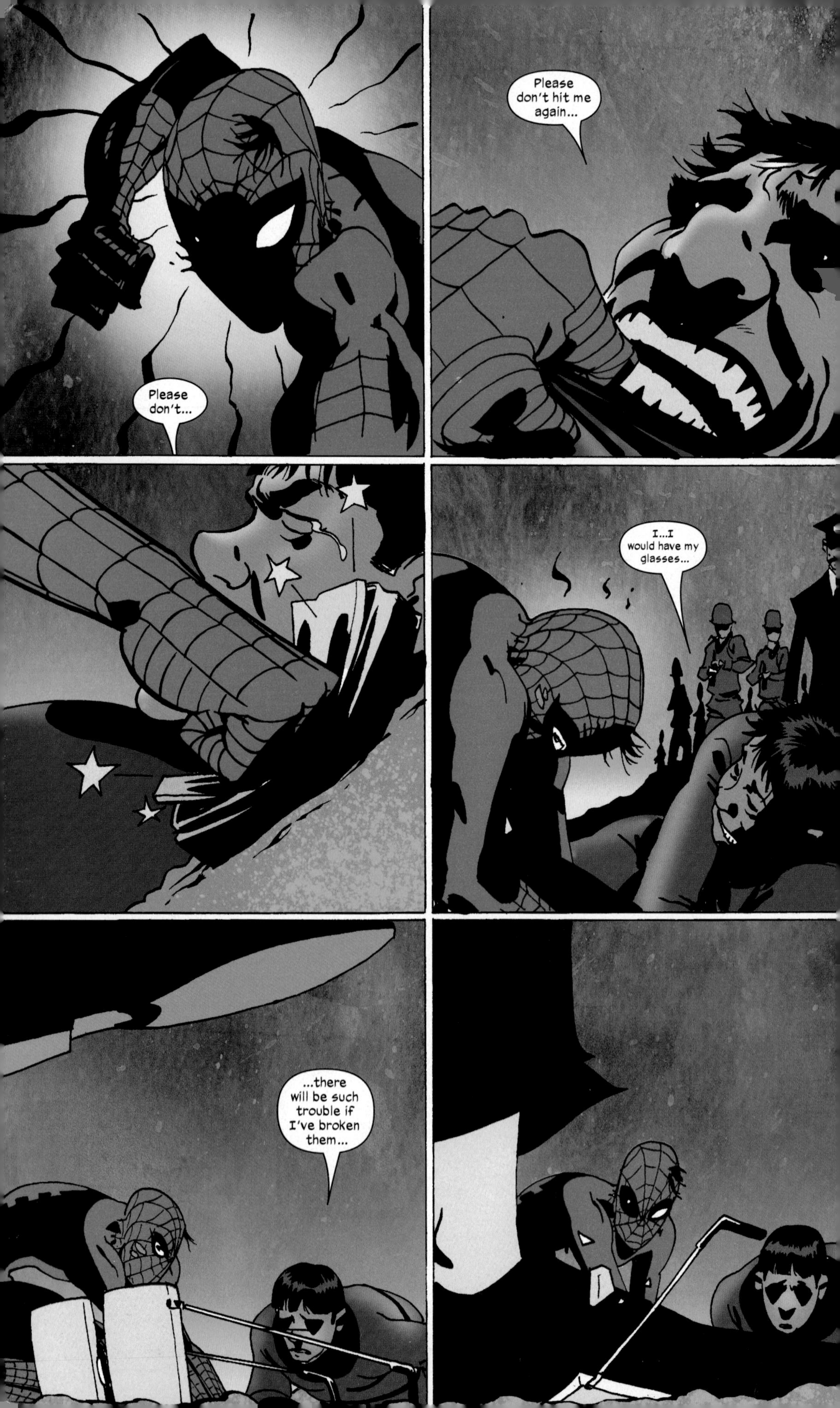
Please don't...
Please don't hit me again...
I...I would have my glasses...
...there will be such trouble if I've broken them...

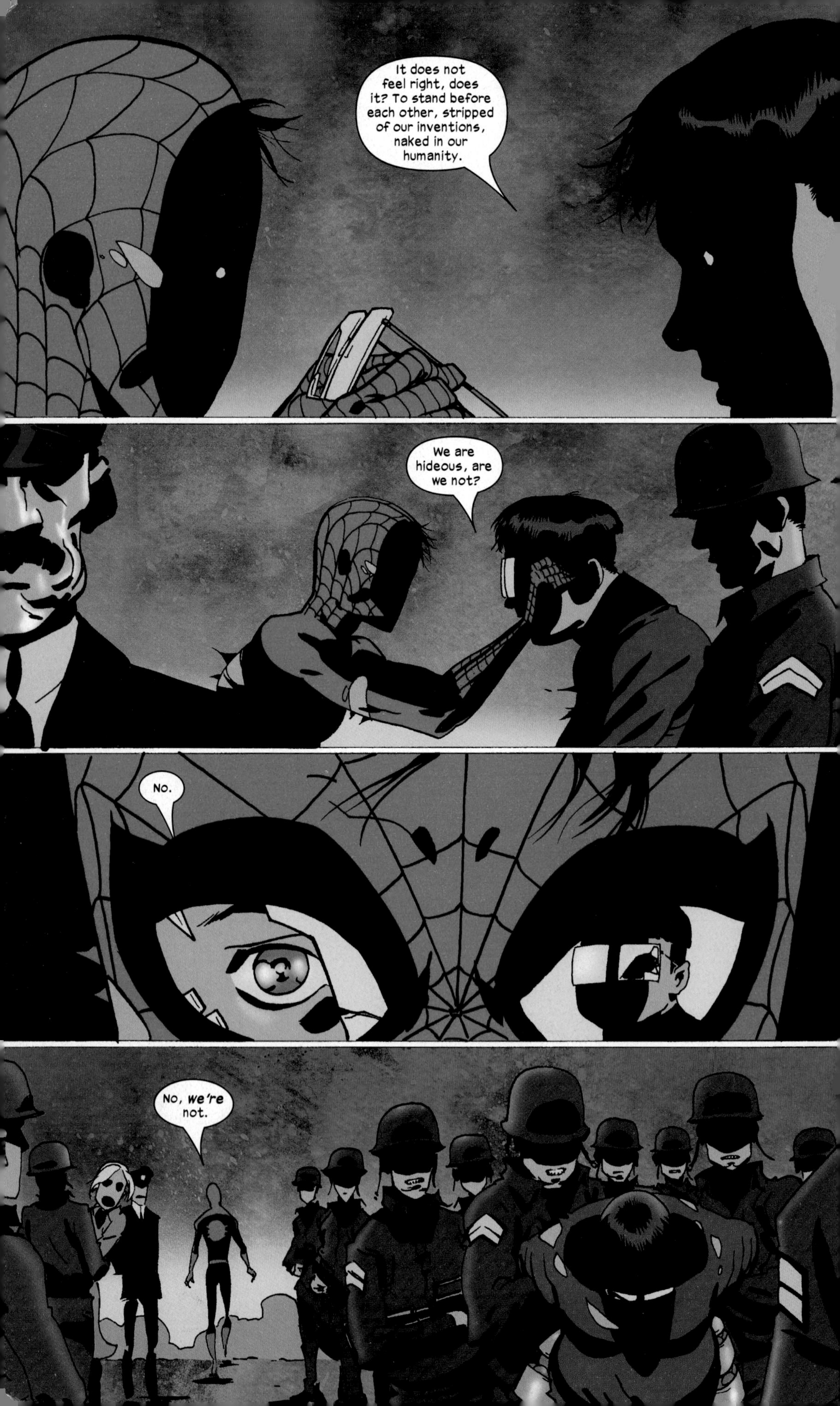
It does not feel right, does it? To stand before each other, stripped of our inventions, naked in our humanity.
We are hideous, are we not?
No.
No, we're not.

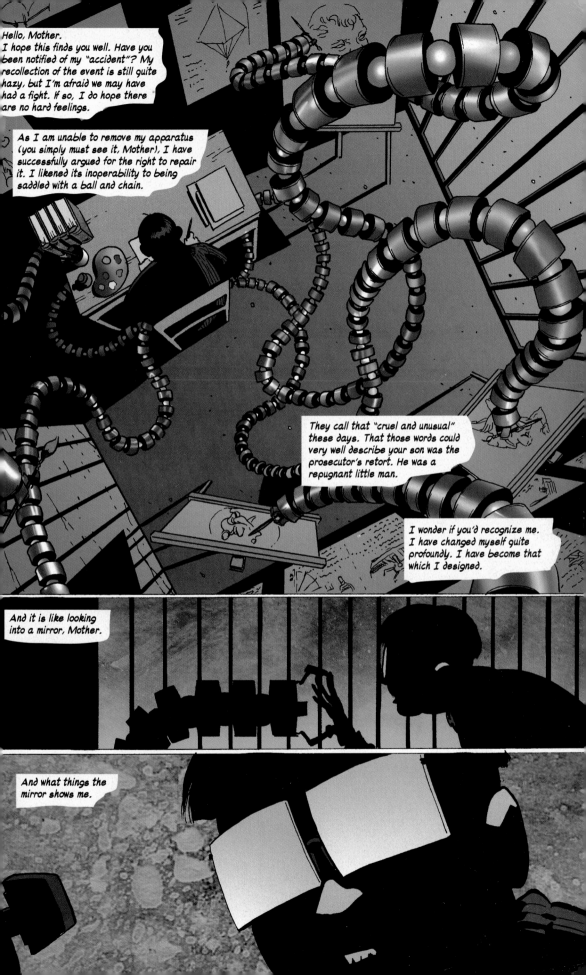

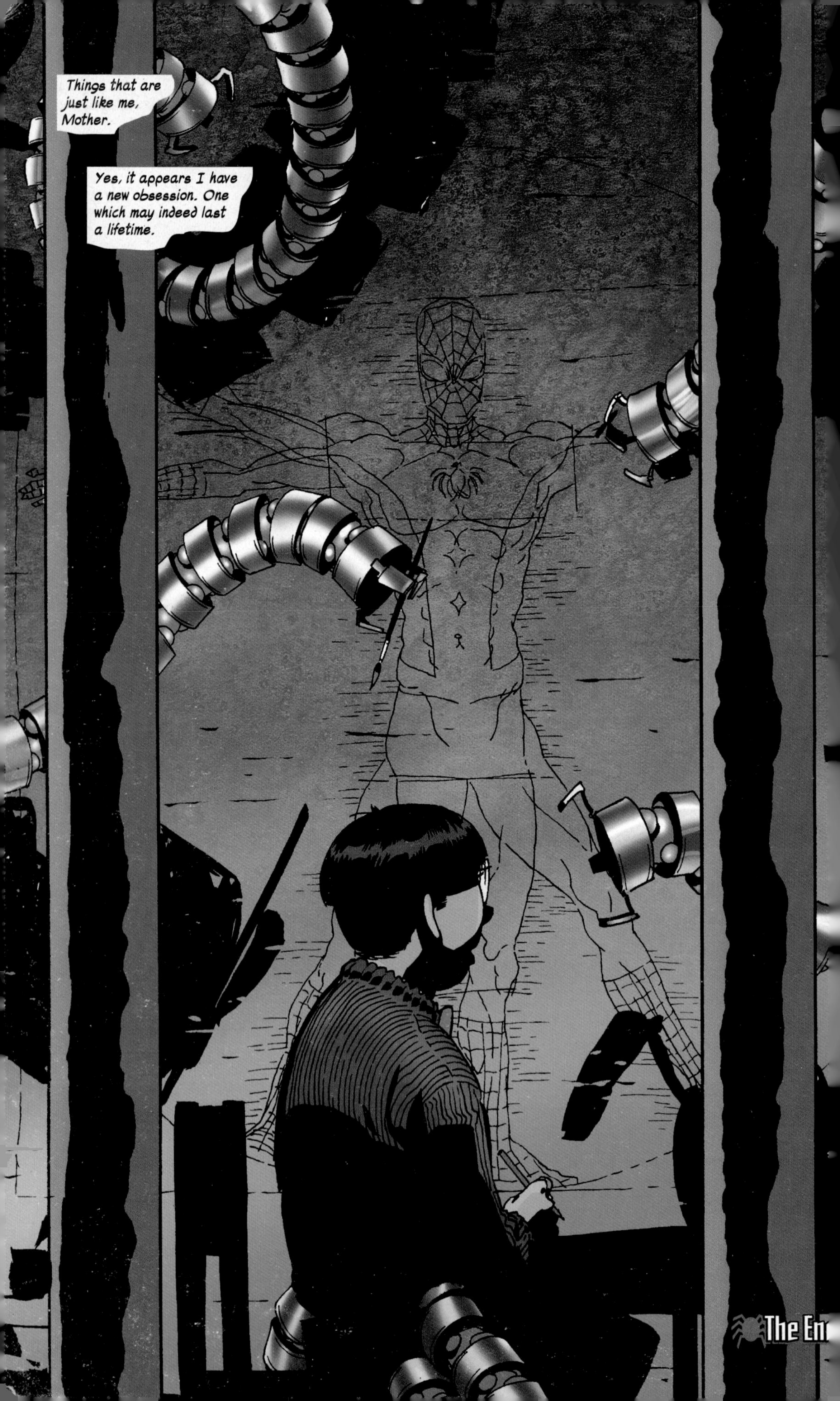
Things that are just like me, Mother.
Yes, it appears I have a new obsession. One which may indeed last a lifetime.
The En